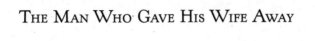

THE MAN WHO GAVE HIS WIFE AWAY

The Man
Who Gave
His Wife
Away

Tom Ireland

ESSAYS

Tres Chicas Books

ACKNOWLEDGMENTS

Some of these essays have been published before. "Fianchetto," "My Thai Girlfriends,"
and "The Pending Disaster" first appeared in *The Missouri Review*; "Past Imperfect"
and "The Woman in Question" in *The Sun*; and "The Man Who Gave His Wife Away"
in the *Santa Fe Literary Review*. In each case, permission to republish is gratefully
acknowledged. Thanks to Evelyn Rogers Somers and Speer Morgan of *The Missouri
Review*. Thanks to Andrew Snee and Sy Safransky of *The Sun*. Thanks to the
National Endowment for the Arts for the opportunity to write "Capitalism" and
"Soledad." Thanks to Miriam Sagan, Joan Logghe, and Renée Gregorio, publishers of
Tres Chicas Books, and to JB Bryan of La Alameda Press. Thanks to Hannah Ireland,
who produced my website, tomireland.net. Thanks to Dirk Kortz. And thanks to
Anne Valley-Fox, who inspired me to put the pieces together.

Cover art :: "The Gallery Series #9" by Dirk Kortz,
30 x 36 inches, 2004, *oil on canvas*

Book design :: JB Bryan

Set in Kennerley

ISBN :: 978-1-893003-14-9

Printed on 100% post-consumer waste recycled paper in accordance with
the Green Press Initiative. The mission of the Green Press Initiative is to work
with publishers, industry, and authors to create paper-use transformations
that will conserve natural resources and preserve endangered forests.

Printed in Canada

Tres Chicas Books
P.O. Box 417
El Rito, New Mexico 87530

For Anne

CONTENTS

Preface

"HUMAN RELATIONSHIPS ARE THE TRAGIC NECESSITY OF HUMAN LIFE," wrote Willa Cather. She wasn't just kidding. You're damned if you do, damned if you don't, and equally blessed either way. Alone, you long for company; in company, you long for the solitude that was just now driving you crazy. Necessity, which has a way of overlooking both the difficulties of relationships and their inevitable loss, keeps us coming back for more in spite of the dependably tragic consequences.

A man says, "I'm through with women." His friend replies, "Me too. Until the next one." We should all have such friends.

"You can't live with them, and you can't live without them," said my father when my mother wasn't listening. Careful with words, he wouldn't have reversed the clauses, which would have soured the sentiment. We would like to be more independent, but our need for *them*, especially *one* of them, eclipses the conflicting impulse.

Spanish makes no distinction between *loneliness* and *solitude*. Both are *soledad*. If you are alone, you are lonely by definition. And if you are lonely, you are also likely to be sad. *Triste*, usually translated as "sad," can also mean "lonely," closing the circle. Perhaps *aloneness*, without its contemporary cast of absence and insufficiency, can be admitted into our lexicon.

Is this about loneliness, or its opposite? How can you know what you are longing for when it has been missing since before you were born?

I may have been lonely at the age of six, but I didn't know it. My parents took note of my solitary nature and tried to make the best of it: "Tommy plays well by himself." Cat's-eye marbles collected from cereal boxes were my artillery. My victims were chess pieces, plastic dinosaurs, toy soldiers, and anything else that could be knocked over and set back on its feet to die again. My father tried to teach me how to shoot marbles with my thumb, the way he'd learned when he was a boy in West Virginia, competing with other boys. I liked my game better. I wasn't playing *alone*, I was just playing, and the play absorbed me for hours on end. As an adult, I've struggled to regain that kind of absorption, just doing or observing, the undivided attention that came so unselfconsciously then.

Loneliness or something like it, an unfamiliar and often frightening anguish, happened the summer I turned ten, at Incarnation Camp—the first time I left home. My way of dealing with it was to crawl into the dark place under the cabin after General Swim, before the dinner bell. I saw the delicate footprints of animals in the dust, but never the animals themselves; the symptoms of this anguish did not lead to its causes. Sometimes I cried; sometimes there was the exultation of knowing that at that very moment, nobody in the world knew exactly where to find me. Thanks to my need for human relationships, I discovered the cool, familiar, and welcoming darkness of solitude, easily accessible only in sleep.

The first journal I ever kept begins with a quotation from Book 13 of William Wordsworth's *Prelude*: "But much was wanting: therefore did I turn to you, ye pathways, and ye lonely roads." I was nineteen, about to leave for a solo cross-country motorcycle tour. My motorcycle buddies had flaked out on me, and anyway, the authentic spirit of Romanticism required that I travel the lonely roads alone. What catches me off balance in that ancient record is not how young and full of myself I was then, which goes without saying—how much in love with the image of the solitary figure on the lake shore, at once dreaming of love and treasuring the anguish of being without it—but how appealing that image still is.

Necessity keeps gaining the upper hand. A friend explains his choice of a mate by saying, "She's the only one who wouldn't go away." Some of the people in these essays have died, and some of them won't go away, but none of them will ever leave entirely. The Lithuanian woman who caught my eye in the rearview mirror one night when I was driving a cab in New York is still there, saying over my shoulder, "You are in love, no? Be always in love, yes."

I call them "essays." "Pieces" might work better except that each piece was written as a whole, without reference to any of the other pieces, and without any prior notion of progression or biographical continuity from one to the next. In its favor, "pieces" reflects life's incoherency, as well as all the empty spaces that fall between those pieces, all the history that has not and will not be written. Inevitably, the individual pieces are full of holes, too.

Most of them were written before I thought of collecting them into a book. More than one reader told me that a book of nonfiction, unlike a book of poems or a novel, for example, needs to be "about" something, so I tried to discover a common theme, one that existed without my prior knowledge. Someone kindly suggested that it was about a "sensibility," the particular spin, whether clarifying or distorting, that the writer had put on his experience. They discerned an underlying tone of melancholy, or longing, that I hadn't been aware of before. But a longing for what? Is it a cop-out to suggest that, like fear, longing doesn't always require a prepositional object, a fear *of* or a longing *for* something?

I often long for something in the presence of other people, even while I'm enjoying their company. I'm longing for the person I am when I'm alone, who unfortunately can't join us. These essays are an attempt to subvert the dilemma. Can their tone of longing, with its implication of distance, pass for a variety of love?

The Sadness after Birth

In sorrow thou shalt bring forth children. — GENESIS 3.16

THEY WERE EATING PANCAKES (or was it waffles?) in the foyer when my mother sat up abruptly at the table and said, "Bernie, I think my water broke! Do something!" Somehow they hustled my sisters off to Aunt Nancy and Uncle Roy's place in Norwalk, Connecticut, before they went to the hospital and had me.

On first seeing his stringbean of a son after the delivery, my father, an old hand at fathering by that time, said "Starvation in India!" He should have known better. My mother burst into tears. It was normal to cry after giving birth, she explained to me years later. They even have a name for it—*post partem triste*—Latin for "the sadness after birth." Many women experience this sadness after having a baby. She had been "vulnerable" at that particular moment, not really sad, at least not in the way people are usually sad. On the contrary, she was completely happy with me, in spite of the tears brought on by my father's wisecrack.

My sister Penny remembers that our mother cried frequently when we were young, presumably "over the frustrations of parenting." It would have been only childlike of us to blame ourselves for her unhappiness. These days, more than twenty years after her death, we're more likely to blame the tiny apartment where we grew up, or the disease—she was diagnosed with Parkinson's when I was in high school—neither of which can defend themselves.

One time I was unquestionably to blame. My parents had gone to the movies, a rare extravagance for them, leaving me and my sisters at home with a friend. With adults on call in the apartment building, my sisters were old enough to look after me without a babysitter. We didn't have a television yet, like the Gutmans upstairs in 3C. The girls hung out in their bedroom doing girl things, which left me to my own evil devices. Whatever made me do it—was I pissed about being abandoned by my parents and ignored by the girls?—I got a knife out of the kitchen drawer and carved my initials in the headboard of my bed. It was one of the few pieces of furniture that my parents owned, made of cherry, which wasn't easy to penetrate with a dull kitchen knife. It only scratched the finish, but enough that anyone could plainly read the letters TSI.

When my parents came home from the movies, my mother put me to bed. She had on perfume that would flavor the room all night while I lay awake, and slept, and woke again to the remnant of her perfume and the unforgiving fact of what I'd actually done, and not just dreamed of doing. It was after she had already kissed me goodnight that she saw the initials scratched in the headboard and said, in a voice unlike any I had ever heard from her before, a voice that she must have been saving for something as awful as this, "Thomas Sparks Ireland. What on earth have you done?"

She seized my wrist but I pulled free and ran down the hall to the bathroom. Before I could get it locked she was pushing from the other side—she was a lot stronger than I would have guessed—and saying in the same terrifying, warlike voice that I had never heard before, "Open the door! I command you to open the door this instant!"

I let go and tried to shelter myself behind the toilet bowl, but she was beyond anger now, and in tears—wilted, defeated, looking at me as if she couldn't believe I was the same son she had given birth to and fed and bathed and worried over when I was sick. In tears, she was much more like herself, the mother I knew, than that other, furious one.

"What possessed you?" was all she could bring herself to say at last, through her tears, as I cowered behind the toilet. "What in God's name possessed you?"

She looked so miserable standing there in her going-to-the-movies dress that I would have given anything not to have done what I had done, or at least to have been able to come up with an answer to her question. Being possessed wasn't the worst because it meant that something beyond my power had taken hold of me and convinced me to do the terrible thing, which wasn't as bad as if I'd done it entirely on my own. But I couldn't say what it was. All I wanted was for her to hit me, which would have been far more merciful than the punishment of seeing her cry.

SHE WAS A PK—A PREACHER'S KID, as such children were known among church people—the daughter of an Episcopalian minister. Born Lois Golder Cline ("That's with a C," she would say, to distinguish it from the multitudinous Kleins of New York). She called her parents Father and Mother and was taught to practice "moderation in all things," a code of behavior that both predicted and enforced a moderate existence, one that constitutionally did not ask for more. Moderation dogged her all her days. Even her death was moderate. She caught double pneumonia and died quickly, without saying good-bye to anyone.

My mother grew up in church rectories—the house that belongs to the church and is occupied by the rector, or parish priest. The word *rector* shares its Latin origin with *rectitude*: straightness, or uprightness. (Isn't it curious how right-handedness, impossible to define except in terms of the side of one's body where the heart is *not*, came to be associated with moral rightness and righteousness, but also with privilege and power?) For being such dedicated church people, my grandparents were never rigid or churchy. My grandfather was known for saying, on the slightest excuse, "Isn't life grand?" He was genuinely convinced that it was, and said so in a way that convinced others of it. His parishioners, his children, and his grandchildren were meant to understand that even a life lived in moderation could be grand.

My mother never took the message completely to heart, or she kept it for a while and then discarded it, having found by then that life was not as grand as it had been cracked up to be. By the time I came along, she was thirty-five—an age at which most women had finished having babies—and must have had some misgivings about starting over from scratch. With the younger of my two sisters, Valerie, about to enter school, she might have chosen to get a job (she was a brilliant typist) or gone back to college—admittedly, options not widely sanctioned then for a married woman with school-age children. (Later on, when I was in school, she took a job as an office assistant at the *Columbia Journalism Review* for a few years, until it became apparent that she wasn't well.) So she had me, whether by design or negligence, her consolation for having to stay home in the little apartment and be what it said she was on my birth certificate: a housewife.

"Housewife" meant she was married to the house, such as it was, with all its "shortcomings." Her word. Quaint biblical or Elizabethan elements surfaced in her vocabulary. "This place looks like a highholder's nest!" she said of an untidy room, something her mother had learned to say from her mother's mother. I've never heard or read the expression anywhere else.

Being married to the house, or in her case the apartment, was analogous in my thinking to being married to Jesus Christ, like the Catholic nuns who lived in a house just down the street and were always walking past our apartment house in their nuns' outfits, on their way to or from church. The nuns and my mother had metaphorical marriages— theirs to Jesus, who had been dead for almost two thousand years; hers to the apartment, which was too small. I had the little bedroom, with a window on a sunless, pigeon-infested airshaft. My sisters had the larger. My parents slept on a foldout couch in the living room, a room without a door, until my sisters left home. When my parents finally claimed the bedroom as their own, they kept my sisters' twin beds, although my father "visited" my mother now and then across the room, by her account, and she put up with him.

She complained bitterly about the kitchen, which took the rap for life's other disappointments. Its physical details are clearer to me than the face of the woman who reluctantly occupied it, with its now legendary inadequacies, from before I was born until well after I went away to college.

As you entered the apartment through the foyer, the kitchen was on the left, behind a door that swung either way, which could be dangerous, as my mother often reminded us. The two-way swinging door was just another failure of her kitchen. The door could have been removed and stored in the basement with the bikes until the next tenants moved in, if anyone were ever to live there again after us, which seemed unlikely. Maybe there was a rule in our apartment house against removing doors.

The kitchen door opened against the Frigidaire, which had to be defrosted. There's my mother, defrosting, food containers stacked on the table. Lifting a pot of boiling water from the stove to be placed in the freezer compartment and loosen the ice that has built up there, which breaks free in white fluted slabs after the steam has weakened it. She's determined to put a quick end to this endless task. Through the kitchen window come the arguments of people in other apartments, their voices magnified by the four enclosing walls of the air shaft, and the smell of their cooking, which smells better than ours.

With room for a table and two chairs, our kitchen couldn't have been all that small by New York standards, but she wanted something better. As a child I had no way of knowing if it was big or small or average compared to other kitchens; I just knew that she hated it. She wasn't much for cooking. How could anyone expect her to get interested in food with a kitchen like that? Cheerios with milk and sugar for breakfast (sliced banana optional). Maybe toast. We weren't eggs and bacon people. She thought that all fried foods were bad for the health. Fried foods made you fat. To compensate for the lack of protein in our breakfast regime, she secretly beat raw egg white into the cereal milk. We weren't fooled. You could see slimy clots of egg white floating around in there among the Cheerios.

There was no cafeteria at P.S. 98, where I went to grade school, so I walked home at noon every day for lunch, across Broadway to the candy store, past the Sacred Heart of Mary where legions of clean Catholic girls skipped rope in their navy uniforms, up the long hill skirting Inwood Hill Park and down the other side. My mother often took the same journey to shop for groceries, pulling a two-wheeled cart down the hill to Grand Union (another example of the plainness of what passed for grandness) and, fully loaded, up the hill again. For this, we declared her heroic.

She was there by herself, in the kitchen, fixing Swiss cheese, mustard, and lettuce sandwiches and chicken noodle soup out of a can. She put out the sandwiches and poured a glass of milk for me and a glass of apple juice for her, diluted with tap water to cut down on the calories. She squeezed in by the window, and I sat at the other end of the table, next to the dangerous door. Between us, next to the toaster, was the radio, which had knobs the color of old people's teeth. We ate our lunch and listened to *Helen Trent*: "Can a woman over 35 find happiness?"

My mother and I didn't talk at lunch when the stories were on. They were one of her few dependable pleasures in life. I listened to Helen's vicissitudes, which were largely incomprehensible. ("What's the big deal? Why can't she just be happy?") I drank my milk, left the dishes on the table, and walked back down the hill to school.

Much of what I know about her has been told to me, rather than remembered, and what I do remember is largely a catalogue of what she was not or could not be.

She didn't go in for parties. Victor and Pearl Marcus, who lived in 3A, came downstairs once in a while to play bridge with my parents in the foyer. She allowed me to sit next to her past my bedtime and look at her hand while she smoked and said things in the language of bridge, which I didn't understand. The point was to sit next to her, and to partake in something, for once, that honestly engaged her. Her lipstick left a red ring on her cigarette.

She had a friend, Portia Clark, who was single and apparently liked being that way. When she lived nearby, Portia came by often to talk, drink, smoke, and listen to music. Sometimes she danced—alone, harem style, crossing her wrists overhead and doing snaky things with her hands. We watched. Portia embodied independence and eccentricity, a way of being alive in the world and its business in a way that was not possible for my mother, for whatever reasons: the apartment, the disease, the confinement of home and family, an incapacity or unwillingness to be or do otherwise. My mother went dutifully to church for our benefit but had no interest in church society. She couldn't tolerate my father's rah-rah college crowd. She didn't want to travel. She didn't drive. She didn't take walks. She was visible, and remains so, mainly by her suffering—although we never called it that. Maybe dissatisfaction, or restlessness, or even something as lively as yearning. But not suffering, at least not until she was diagnosed with Parkinson's, a disease of the brain, the lack of some vital chemical, which redeemed her suffering to the extent of giving it a proper name. As her children grew up and left home, she grew smaller and less substantial, a phantom in bedroom slippers padding up and down the hallway with a bowl of coffee ice cream.

She always griped about being fat, but she was really just soft, as if she were missing some important bones. She wore a girdle when she went out, which made her feel thinner, and nylon stockings, which were fastened to the girdle with padded clasps at the end of elastic strips. She kept grocery money there, too, in a silk purse held in place by the nylons. Her physical vigor stayed in hiding unless called forth by dire necessity. When I was sick, she shook the mercury down with such violent whips of her wrist that I was afraid the thermometer might fly out of her hand and break on the floor. She could be convinced to play croquet with us on the wide lawn at Aunt Nancy and Uncle Roy's place in Woodbridge, Connecticut, swinging the mallet girl style, between her legs, although she wore only skirts, which got in the way of her swing—never shorts or slacks. She usually preferred to sit in a lawn chair during these games and cheer for whoever was losing.

I thought her pretty in a vulnerable way, with her mother's sad-dog eyes, thickly lidded at the corners, and that same expression of compassionate intelligence and reserve, combined, that I saw in a portrait of my grandmother, born Lois Golder Clute, whom she'd been named after. The Clute nose was nothing other than refined, evidence that my mother's people had once enjoyed a higher place in society and that she deserved better than what she got. My mother's nose conveyed *hauteur*, or would have, had she been able to keep up the appearances of her aristocratic past, although that haughtiness could reassert itself when she had to put up with strangers who lacked her natural-born refinement. When the plumber fixed the bathroom sink and left behind his greasy fingerprints, she called him "coarse."

Photographs of her are not unbecoming, although she didn't like having her picture taken. Here she looks about six, round-cheeked, professionally posed in a white organdy Easter dress with an enormous white satin bow in her hair, the face unsmiling yet unperturbed, obedient to the occasion. The photographer knew better than to ask her to smile. Here she's sitting on a bench with my father when they were recently engaged or married. He has the look in his eye, and she's playing hard to get, shying away from him as he leans insistently in her direction, one simian fist planted on the bench between them. They are obviously in love, and obviously playing the part of being in love for the camera. How did they meet? She had dated a professional hockey player, and a church organist who invited her to his place to see his organ (that was the end of that), and she was seeing someone else when my father showed up and took command, but nobody can tell me exactly where or how that happened. Next thing you know, they're "making a little ecstatically blissful wogo-pogo on the sly" in Fort Tryon Park, as my father wrote in his journal, and talking about their coming marriage—"the pending disaster."

Here she's on a cruise ship on the St. Lawrence River, perhaps the only time they ever took a vacation together, just the two of them. Beyond, a milky vastness of sky and water. She's been instructed to stand next to the ship's wheel, which she holds ever so gently, touching the spokes like the strings of a harp. She's wearing sunglasses, and she seems to be saying something: go ahead, what are you waiting for, take it. And here she is in Woodbridge, presenting herself to the picture taker in a new fall coat, as red as it can be. Hair newly done. The palms of her hands lifted, arms held extravagantly away from her sides, as if she has just walked on stage. She's almost pleased with herself.

Parkinson's was not a "terminal" disease, they said, but it weakened you over time until you became vulnerable to other diseases. When my mother was diagnosed, an unusual excitement entered our lives for a while, like the excitement that happens when someone is born or dies. The importance newly conferred on her made the rest of us more important, too. Now I was a young man whose mother had a dreadful and incurable disease, calling for qualities that I wasn't sure I possessed. Compassion. Sacrifice. Courage. Portia, my mother's friend, said that my mother needed me now; I needed to "be there for her." But I had been there all along, even before that sweltering day in July 1946 when her water broke in the foyer and she and I went to Sloane Hospital and regarded each other face to face for the first time. How could I be there for her any more than I already was?

In the years before she got sick, my mother played the piano—a fact I might have mentioned before naming the many things she could not be or do, except that her weaknesses still hold such stubborn sway in memory. Whether at the piano or the typewriter, or hanging clothes on a clothesline, she was good with her hands: she was *dexterous* (Latin again, that old bias in favor of the right, even though everybody knows that playing the piano and typing take two equally clever hands). She taught me to touch-type by covering the keys of the Underwood with adhesive tape, which forced me to keep my eyes on the workbook. (To this day I can smell adhesive tape when I'm typing.) When I was still in grade school we bought an upright piano, the only kind that would fit through the door, with keys that looked as if they had been seared in a fire. Raw wood showed through the finish where it had scraped against stairwells and door frames. She was amazed that she could still play, and I was amazed that she could play at all. Show tunes, especially Rodgers and Hart. She talked me into singing along while she played, a service performed grudgingly that I secretly loved. I sat beside her on the piano bench. When she bobbed her head, that was the signal to turn the page. "My Funny Valentine," with its ironic message about love and beauty. "Is your figure less than Greek? Is your mouth a little weak?" Debussy's "Gollywog's Cakewalk" made her hands leap back and forth across the keyboard and land roughly. She struggled with it for a while until it reduced her to tears. Her hands, which had always been so quick, would no longer do what she wanted them to do. The lid came down on the keyboard, the sheet music went back into the bench for storage, and except when I played "Woodland Waltz," the piano went untouched for years until the movers took it away.

My mother was one of the first to receive L-dopa, a drug made from the brains of fish, we learned, that helped control the tremors of Parkinson's. Doctors were always busy adjusting her various medications, up and down, on and off, so that she sometimes didn't know if her feelings were her own, or chemically manufactured, or if it really mattered which was which. Years later, in a rush of manic energy, she invited a bunch of people over to the apartment for a double engagement party for me and Valerie, and when it was already too late to call things off, realized with horror what she had done. After the party, an occasion memorable for its intergalactic silences, both engagements were broken off.

We blamed the drugs. She took Elavil for "depression"—a word that I'd never heard in connection with my mother before she was diagnosed with Parkinson's. It lifted her mood, but the dose had to be carefully regulated, especially since she took other prescription drugs along with it, leading to unpredictable side effects. If Elavil had inspired her to throw a party, there was no telling what other macabre behavior it might lead to.

The initial excitement of our family disaster wore off, and we were left with nothing more than a sick, depressed woman. The doctors and the medications they prescribed could suppress the symptoms but do nothing about the disease itself, a debt that could never be paid down no matter how long she lived. I could say that she was never herself again. Far from it, knowledge of the disease made her more like herself than ever, at least the one that I had come to know: morose, retiring, and lacking in any apparent ambition other than to keep the apartment in order, take her medications, watch television, and fall asleep with a fat novel turned upside down on her breast.

These were qualities, if they can be called that, that I know only too well in myself and have tried to trace to their family origins, for where could they have originated but in the family? She began a slow descent into listlessness, resignation, self-pity, despair. It was as if by naming her sickness the doctors had given her permission to be sick, which was the allowance she had been waiting for. Now at least she had an identity other than "housewife," although by that time she had adopted the more fashionable "homemaker." As an invalid, or one who could reasonably expect to become one as the disease ran its course, she no longer had to make the tiresome effort that it took to live, as opposed to merely going through the motions of living. Her new job was to eat fish brains and remind us piously that if you had your health, you had everything.

How could I, her beloved and loving son, have let it happen? Destructive forces were being allowed to take over my mother's mind and body, and all of us, doctors and family, were complicit in her demise. We gave it a name and a position of honor. We sanctified it.

I WENT TO COLLEGE, then to graduate school in California, then to practice meditation at a commune in New Mexico. My mother and I communicated infrequently in letters. She watched the weather reports on TV and took particular note of what was happening atmospherically wherever I happened to be. When I wrote a book, she responded favorably: "I like the way you write. You don't use too many words." A good son, upholding the tradition of moderation in all things.

One time I was home for the holidays. My mother and I were in their bedroom, which had been my sister's bedroom. Without a fire escape, it had a good view of Park Terrace West—the street's cobblestones had only recently been tarred over—where it drops steeply to 218th Street. On icy winter mornings it had been entertaining to stand by that window and watch cars spin out of control on the hill and narrowly miss or, better yet, hit the cars parked on either side, like a colossal pinball game.

She asked me if I had any girlfriends, which was strange, because she'd never questioned me about that sort of thing before, or offered any opinion about what one could expect or not expect from love. I told her that I'd taken up with one woman in the commune and then left her to go live in a cave and "be by myself," but there were fleas in the cave, and I'd taken up with another woman, and when that happened the first woman had gone away to be by *herself* and was living with an artist in a nearby village, supposedly as his apprentice.

"Sounds like she's got the inside track," my mother said, in the mysterious way that mothers have of knowing things about their children that the children don't know or will not admit.

"Well, however it works out, I wish you great joy in life, and great sadness."

An eccentric wish for a mother to make for her only son, a blessing and a curse all rolled into one, and it didn't make much sense then. But it did later on, after I'd done some more living of my own. She was giving me the gift of independence, of having all the consequences of a life fully lived, and not just the happy ones. It didn't really matter which it was, joy or sadness, as long as it was great.

My grandfather gave me a bible for a confirmation present. When he died, in 1968, I had just finished college and was about to leave home for real, to put some serious distance between me and them for the first time. In leaving I had the biblical example of the Prodigal Son to follow, the one who refuses to keep on the straight and narrow, leaves home for a distant land, disassociates himself spiritually from the tribe and whatever he believes it represents—in my case, complacency, security at the expense of freedom, work done for the sake of mere survival (who needs it?) and its ultimate letdown, retirement. We were New Testament folks. The parable of the wayward child, who is loved more for having gone away and returned than the son who stays at home with his nose to the grindstone, suited me better than the stern Old Testament model: "In the sweat of thy face shalt thou eat bread, till thou return to the ground." Sick or well, my mother needed me; sick or well, she also needed me to go away and find my way in the world, which is what sons were supposed to do. (Daughters were another matter.) My father had left the farm on the spur of the moment, applying to college in August and starting classes in September. He rarely saw his family of origin after that, and we, his children, saw them even less. His relatives remained creatures of myth, distinguished mainly by their austerities or their bizarre deaths: his Methodist mother who, unlike us, actually *read* the Bible; the natural father he never knew (wasn't he the one who died when his car was hit by a train?); the great-aunt who choked to death on a wheat straw; the cousin who left his wife for another woman and had a bastard baby with her, the closest we'd ever come to downright waywardness. Sad stories made grotesque by our remove from them, whereas our own sad stories were simply sad.

I left, though not nearly as completely as my father had when he made the mighty leap into college and the middle class. Airplanes made it nearly impossible not to visit. After my father retired, they moved into a new apartment in Connecticut, somewhat more spacious and much newer than what they'd had in New York. It had tennis courts for my father, and beyond the parking lot, a view of fields that had not yet been taken over by developers, where real vegetables were grown. Cabbages! Those humdrum things of my father's youth, fields and crops, which he had gone to such lengths to escape, had finally become the object of his wonder and admiration. The new apartment had a bright, roomy kitchen with modern appliances, which my mother conceded was "adequate."

The L-dopa had spared her from the worst of Parkinson's symptoms. She was weak, but every now and then the best parts of her nature would come through: a wry skepticism, a sense of life's absurdity, outbreaks of determination (in former times she had been downright pushy in department stores when other shoppers got in her way), qualities largely obscured by the veil of the disease.

We were having cocktails in the living room when I told them the story of my Selective Service physical in California. I have a hammertoe, the second toe on my left foot, which curls back under itself and grows a toenail like a barnacle. I tried to get exempted from military service because of this toe—I didn't want to go to war in Vietnam if there was any way of avoiding it—but at the physical the doctor only laughed and said, "You've got to be kidding. You call that a hammertoe? You ought to see my grandmother. Now *she* has a hammertoe!"

27

"What are you talking about?" said my mother. "You've got a hammertoe?"

"Sure, you knew that."

"I knew no such thing. Let me see it."

So I took off my shoe and sock and showed her the toe. She looked at it, and handled it tenderly, and shook her head. "No," she said. "No, you didn't have that when you were born. I remember very well. When the nurse brought you, I looked you over carefully, and there wasn't a thing wrong with you. Not a thing." Here she gave my father a dirty look. "As far as I was concerned, you were a perfectly beautiful baby."

The Violin in the Closet

"Why are you doing this?" she asked when I came to her apartment for the first lesson. Her name was Cynthia. She was very blonde, and so pale that her skin looked faintly blue, like skim milk.

"Hard to say, exactly. But it may be a matter of life and death."

She showed me how to hold the violin and bow, that is, how not to hold but to balance them. She poked my hand and elbow into place, twisted my head around with a rusty-hinge squeak. At the end of the hour she ripped the week's assignment from a steno pad and handed it to me.

"See you next time. That is, if you decide to continue."

"I'll be here."

"Great. Bring an assignment book."

"And the violin?"

When she smiled, her neck and face darkened. "That would be helpful."

Up early the next morning, I had to walk around the neighborhood to burn off some of the surplus excitement. I wanted to skip all the preliminaries and jump right into Bach's partitas and sonatas for solo violin. Returning to the cold and dark of my apartment, I saw the bowl of tangelos on the counter. I could smell them, too! It had been more than a year since I'd really seen or smelled anything.

No time for breakfast. I got out the violin, and before the sun had risen well into the sky, I had the first measure of "Tennessee Waltz" by heart.

Molly and I had split up after ten years of marriage and agreed to share the upbringing of our daughter Hannah, who turned six that summer. Everything was to be as close to fifty-fifty as possible. Instead of the usual school-and-summer division of child care, Hannah went back and forth between Molly's place and mine on a complicated but fair schedule, so that no season of the year was owned by one parent or the other. When she was living with Parent A, she spent the weekends with Parent B, and vice versa. It was a good system in almost every respect, except that she was gone half the time.

I had a second death to contend with that October. Two days after I told him the news of the separation, my father fell dead in his apartment in Connecticut. He was alone. A chair had been knocked over—he may have been trying to reach the phone. On his desk was a letter addressed to me, sealed and stamped, that he hadn't lived long enough to mail. He was sorry that "two such wonderful people" had to suffer—as if our better natures could save us from suffering. The single life wasn't easy, he wrote. (My mother had died two years earlier.) But he was confident that in the long run, I'd be "stronger" for what I had to go through.

I wasn't so sure.

Molly was given the violin on the condition that she, or someone else, actually play it. Instead she took up the cello and asked me if I wanted the violin. Maybe this was just the thing to take my mind off my troubles—a project so demanding that it would make me forget about everything else.

I wrote book reviews for the newspaper, took construction jobs, and eventually got rated by the federal government to edit an architectural study of the missions of San Antonio, Texas—my first desk job ever. In the basement of an airless government building I read the long, tedious manuscript on the green screen of an IBM Displaywriter. One of the early Spanish missionaries had politely called the mission outhouse "el lugar de la necesidad secreta," the place of secret necessity. Such a place surely had to exist, at least in consciousness, if one were patient and attentive enough to find it.

When my job with the feds ended, there was nothing to do but look for work and practice the violin. I let my beard grow and warmed my fingers with cups of hot water, supposedly something Isaac Stern did before going on stage.

I had a knack for finding cold, dark places to live. This one, a detached studio behind the landlord's house, was the coldest and darkest yet. Mildew thrived on the walls. It had a make-believe kitchen and a miniature bathtub that forced me to take one bath from the waist up, feet pointed at the ceiling, and another from the waist down. The landlord, Dietegen, didn't flinch when I told him that I was learning the violin. After all, he was German, and all Germans loved music.

Cynthia didn't laugh at my noise-making. Now and then she demonstrated on the viola. That such a big, rich sound could be produced by someone so pale and delicate didn't seem plausible. The viola had the violin's sweetness, but it had that low-down coarseness, too, as if particles of silence had lodged between the particles of sound. Her face changed when she played; she removed to regions I might never visit, much less inhabit. I had to keep reminding myself to watch what she was doing instead of watching her.

After the first of the year, Hannah moved back with her mother during the week. Without her there to feed and clothe and taxi to school and back, I felt all but useless. She had turned seven the previous summer. What did it mean to her that, all of a sudden, both her parents were mad for music? Where once she had complained about not having brothers or sisters, now she complained about having to compete with two other siblings for attention—the cello and the violin.

Cynthia was standing right in front of me with her arms folded across her exquisite chest. How did she expect me to concentrate on the exercise with her in the line of vision?

"Try to keep your chin on the chin rest. Keep your spine and hips straight. Feet a little farther apart. That's it. Now use the whole bow. Long, slow strokes. Start at the frog and play slowly all the way to the tip and then back to the frog. The motion is to the side, like casting seed into a furrow. That's better. Don't worry about the left hand right now, we'll work on that later. Good. Very nice."

After the lesson we sat on the couch while she wrote out the assignment. She didn't seem to mind my sitting next to her and looking over her shoulder.

"You seem awfully tense," she said. "Your playing will improve a lot faster if you can learn to relax during the lesson. I know, it's not easy. I always hated lessons."

"I'll never be able to relax until you have dinner with me," I tried.

She stopped writing, placed the notebook on the coffee table, and left the room without a word. After a long minute she returned with a calendar.

"How's next Wednesday?" she said.

"Great. Are you a vegetarian? I'm in the mood for some raw red meat."

On Wednesday we drove to a steak restaurant outside of town and drank a lot of wine, which, along with first-date nerves, made me extraordinarily talkative.

"It's not craft that interests me," I went on. "Real art means doing what you want to do, while so much that passes for art consists of doing what you expect will please others. We want so badly to go naked but we keep putting on new costumes to conceal our nakedness. Everything I need to know is already in me, waiting to be revealed. That's where you come in."

"Let me get this straight. You want me to strip you naked?"

"Something like that, yes."

We were eating desert, a syrupy flan. I was wearing a silk paisley tie that I'd bought the day before at a second-hand store and was doing my best to keep it out of the flan.

"Don't move," she said. She reached across the table, grabbed the tie, reeled me in, and gave me her syrupy mouth.

Another Sunday night. I was driving Hannah across town to drop her off at Molly's. Weekends always went by fast, but they went by even faster knowing that I had to give her up again come Sunday night. Her struggles remained mostly unspoken, and whenever I tried to unlock them, the silence only grew. Large seven-year-old resentment was being held there, but towards what or whom?

"How's Molly?" I said.

"Fine."

"How's she doing with her cello?"

"Good."

"Does she practice a lot?"

"Not too much."

"Is she still with what's-his-name?"

"Ken."

"Do you like him?"

"Yeah, he's nice."

We turned on Placita del Oro and passed the coin-op car wash. All the bays were empty. In three months, when school was out, she would come to live with me again during the week. Three months seemed a terribly long time, but it would pass. Then I'd be missing her on the weekends.

"I gave up eating candy for Ash Wednesday," she announced as we pulled into Molly's driveway.

"I thought you didn't eat candy. How can you give up something that you don't eat anyway?"

She shrugged. "It was easy."

"I'm not going to sleep with you tonight," Cynthia announced outside her apartment after our third date. We were having a late February thaw, and her landlord had spread a truckload of two-inch gravel over the mud that hurt my feet through the soles of my shoes.

"No?"

"No. I need a little more time."

"I've got time. But it sounds like you *want* to sleep with me."

"Is that a question or a statement?"

"Both."

"Yes. The answer to the question you didn't ask is yes. But a girl's got to have some principles. Or appear to."

"What principles?"

"Never sleep with your student before he's mastered a two-octave G-major scale with a turnaround."

"Okay. I'll work on that."

"Do you want to come in?"

"Better not. I've got principles, too."

"Like what?" She reached up and clasped her hands behind my neck.

"I forget."

The roof in my apartment continued to leak. At night the sound of water dripping into buckets kept me awake—that, and the thought of my dwindling savings. When you came in the door, the first thing you saw was the exercise book on its stand. Someone was home and seriously occupied. I called it "the music room." Hannah called it "the family room."

I practiced between three and five hours every day. Out of clean clothes, I drove downtown to the Adobe Laundromat and started two loads. If the traffic wasn't too bad, I drove home, practiced for ten minutes, and arrived at the Adobe just before the spin cycle ended. I put the clean wash in the dryer and plugged in forty minutes worth of dimes. That gave me fifteen minutes with the violin before it was time to go back and fold.

Dietegen came to look at the roof. "It's very dark in here. I think it would be good to put in a couple of skylights. That will brighten it up. I can fix the roof at the same time." He looked at the music on the stand. "This is what you are all the time playing?"

"Henry Purcell. English. He died young, like Mozart."

"Ah, Purcell. Is it very difficult?"

"For me, yes."

"The blonde woman who comes here with the violin. She is your teacher?"

"Yes. She's a violist."

"Nice looking. She looks German."

"Her ancestors were German."

"You and she are . . . ?"

"We're lovers, yes."

"This is not a problem when your teacher is also your lover?"

"Not yet, anyway. I got interested in the violin before I got interested in her."

"Who cares?" said Dietegen. "Love is the important thing. You love the woman. You love the violin. Don't try to understand."

The Purcell had me buffaloed. I couldn't put five decent notes together, and I dreaded playing those high notes on the E string, where my bad intonation was magnified. And as soon as I got up any speed or length in the bow, the violin started making insect noises.

"You've got a high-strung bow," said Cynthia when I called. "It was made for an accomplished player."

"What you're telling me in a nice way is that my bow's too good for me."

"Or not good enough."

"Maybe it doesn't sound as bad as I think it does."

"Sorry. These things are not subjective. I want you to try my bow for a while and see if it makes a difference. Just don't teach it any bad habits."

It was a beauty, with silver-wire wrapping and an ebony frog with mother-of-pearl inlay. And at least to my ear, it sounded far better than mine.

"Please measure the bow speed so each quarter note gets as much bow as the next. Don't use up the frog so fast. Not so much arm. Elbow and wrist. We want follow-through. We want a beautiful, fluid, lyrical bow."

The telephone rang in the bedroom. When she returned I was sitting on the couch and the violin was in its case.

"You're sulking," she said.

"Why do you have to talk to me that way?"

"What way?"

"Like your student."

"You *are* my student."

"I know, but you don't have to talk to me like one. 'We want a beautiful, fluid, lyrical bow.' It's condescending."

"How am I supposed to talk to you?"

"I don't know. I have a tender ego. I don't like being told what to do."

"That's what teachers do. If you don't like it, you shouldn't have a teacher. Not me, anyway."

"Okay. Let's try it again. Tell me what to do."

She climbed on top of me, her knees on either side of mine, and forced me to look her in the eye.

"Keep my bow for a while," she said. "It won't correct your action, but it sounds a hell of a lot better than yours. And one other thing."

"Maestro?"

"Love me. Can you handle that?"

In the dirt border next to the walkway, Hannah helped me plant peas, garlic, flax, daisies, and bluebonnets in the wet ground. The curtains parted for the first time in months, and light fought its way into the studio. With it came stirrings of something I was afraid to admit or to name. Ghostlike, it might vanish as suddenly as it had appeared if concentrated attention were brought to it.

When school was over, Hannah moved back with me during the week. On her eighth birthday, we hung streamers in "the family room." She wanted to leave them up after the party, and to keep from snagging them with the bow I moved to the rear of the studio. The sound wasn't as lively back there, and the ceiling was so low that I had to aim my up-bows between the roof beams. Hannah went to the Girls Club every day, where a semblance of organized fun concealed a fundamental chaos. If no children were missing at the end of the day, it was considered a success. I picked her up at four and we drove home.

"What did you do today?"

"Not much."

If she was blaming me for something, I would have preferred her blame to her silence. As it was, I couldn't figure out where to start. How could I have failed to see that she was just as worried about me as I was about her, and that what I saw as her unhappiness was largely a reflection of my own?

"What would you think if Cynthia and I decided to live together?" I asked her one night after putting her to bed.

"Where will I live?"

"With us, of course. And part of the time with Molly, just the way it is now. We'd have to find another house to live in. You'd have your own room. You could learn to play a musical instrument, and we could all play music together."

"Which instrument will I play?"

"How about the clarinet? You look like a clarinet player to me."

I kissed her good night and pulled the privacy blanket closed.

"Tom?" she called a few minutes later. I wanted to be "Dad" but had never gotten it to stick.

"What?"

"I think I want to play the drum."

"That's a good idea. Now go to sleep."

Cynthia and I were lying in bed. The heat of the summer had come. There was no way to turn off the security light outside her bedroom window. It made everything blue.

"Did you ever hear about the ceremony that married couples perform in Indonesia?" I said. "Maybe it's not Indonesia, but someplace like that. Once a year, the man and woman stand back to back, and either one of them can walk away from the other, and then they're not married anymore. And if neither one of them walks away, then they're committed to each other for another year. They don't talk about it, the way we do in this country. They just walk away, or they don't, and either way everyone's cool with it, even the in-laws."

"Who says they're cool?"

"That's the way they are. It's sanctioned by the society at large."

"Just because it's sanctioned by the society doesn't mean they're cool with it."

"Maybe not. I just thought it was a neat way of keeping things honest."

"What are you trying to tell me?" she said. She was lying on her side with one hand propped under her head. Her hair, her breasts, her whole body was blue. "What does this have to do with you and me, exactly?"

"Nothing. I'm not talking about you and me. You have to make a commitment to someone before you can break it."

In July I left Hannah with her mother and drove east for a vacation. At a campground in Kansas, nighthawks breached the air at dusk. I set up the portable music stand and played until it was too dark to see. Friends in Missouri tolerated the man who practiced in the sweltering heat of their living room, a good houseguest who declined to run the air conditioning while they were at work. At my sister's cabin in Wisconsin, I played with a mute to keep from disturbing the household and fought off wasps with Cynthia's bow. How wonderful to play with seagulls drifting near, and the sound of water falling gently against land, and sand under your feet!

One night I dreamed an effortless vibrato. My left hand moved with its own life. In the dream I couldn't avoid perfection any more than, in waking life, I could keep from making mistakes. A rich, pulsing tone issued from the violin. The violinist had no fear.

By the time I returned to New Mexico, it was August. Cynthia did not try to avoid the issue. She'd had a fling with a horn player who was in town for the chamber music festival. When she told me I hit the table with my fist—the right one, my bow hand.

"What the hell were you thinking?" I said.

"I didn't think you cared that much one way or the other."

"Of course I care. What do you think this is all about? The violin?"

"Before you left you said we didn't have a commitment to break. Remember?"

"I wasn't talking about us. I was talking about the Indonesians. If other people want to live that way, it's up to them. But I'm not like that.

For Christ's sake, Cynthia, a horn player? What is he, a trombonist?"

"French horn."

"I should have known."

"Do you love him?"

"No. I love you. That's what *I* should have known."

I'd hurt my hand when I hit the table and couldn't play—that, or I didn't have the heart for it. Molly and I got our signals crossed and I was trapped at home one Sunday afternoon waiting for Hannah to be delivered. Any other time, a whole afternoon at home alone would have been ecstasy, a time for undistracted practice. Now it was a sentence to be served. I took a walk in the neighborhood to let off some steam. Black clouds were piling up over the mountains. It was the season of hailstorms and shooting stars. On the way home I found a ten dollar bill lying on the street. It was the ten dollars I owed Cynthia from our last lesson, before I'd gone on vacation.

"I've got some money for you," I told her on the phone.

"You're quitting."

"No, I'm not quitting. When's my next lesson?"

"Thursday. How's your hand?"

"Okay, I guess. I haven't tried it out yet."

"If you can, work on those triplets in the Sevcik. And the bowing. Watch yourself in the mirror."

"That might be difficult. I'm not exactly a pretty sight these days."

On Thursday I rushed through the exercises while she paced. "Slow down those eighths! Let the music breathe! It's all choked off!"

"What the hell did you expect?" I threw the violin on the couch and went outside. I wanted to see the stars. She came and stood next to me and took hold of my arm.

"What's up there?" she said.

"Nothing. It's too bright here. You can't see a damn thing."

"I think we should can the lesson and go to bed."

"I've got a better idea. Let's get a bottle and go to the dump."

With blankets, pillows, a bottle of mescal, a bag of corn chips, and a boiled artichoke, we drove west into the hills at the edge of town and pulled off the road. The ground was covered with broken glass from other people's parties. We climbed into the bed of the pickup and pulled the blankets over us.

"We're at the tail end of the Perseids," I said. "If we're lucky, we might see a shooting star."

"What are they shooting at?"

The mescal tasted like railroad ties. Cynthia tasted like Cynthia. I told her that I wanted her to live with me.

"I think that's a good idea," she said.

"Hannah wants to play the drums. We'll have a trio."

We ate the artichoke and watched for meteors. There were a few faint streaks in the northeast, but nothing to get excited about.

After a while she said, "I will not live with anyone who plays the drums."

Something ample, warm, flooded with light. A practice room looking out on a garden, a wooden floor under my feet to act as a sounding board for the instrument. A whitewashed room on the shore of the Aegean would do just fine.

"After forty, you have to decide what you really want to do," said Dietegen. His head hung upside down through the coffin-shaped hole that he'd just cut through the roof. He'd finally started on the skylights after I told him that Cynthia and I were looking for a place together. "The one thing you can't live without. Nobody can do everything in one life, am I right? So you have to do the one thing that is the most important."

"What's the most important thing for you?"

"There's a mountain in Argentina with my name on it. But in between climbs, what am I?"

Cynthia and I looked at one house with plenty of floor space but not enough head room. My bow would scrape the ceiling. Another one, on San Antonio Street, fell short of my Aegean villa, but it had a laundry room with a view of a walled garden. I could practice outside until the weather turned cold. The ceramic sun-faces on the stucco wall never stopped smiling. Hannah had a carpeted room next to ours—no window, but a regulation room with a door. She and Cynthia played gin rummy in the evening while the dishwasher went through its paces. It was almost like being a family.

Cooking oil had spilled on Cynthia's bow during the move, and I took it to be rehaired. They shined the silver, too, and put a piece of surgical rubber on the grip to give me a better hold. A couple brought in the wreckage of their son's cello while I was there. When they'd left, the man behind the counter said, "He used it for a pogo stick."

My first student concerto, Schubert's "Impromptu," arrived in the mail just after we moved into the new house. I opened to the piano part first . . . how the hell was I supposed to play three notes at once? When Cynthia played it on the viola, I wept.

"My mother used to play that on the piano," I said.

"When you play it, she'll be listening."

During the first lesson at the new house, we played a duet, Bartok's "Cushion Dance." The beginning was rough. I kept misreading the first note, wanting it to be a C-sharp instead of what Bartok had written, a simple open A, and we had to keep starting over. Cynthia's patience was hard to swallow. Why this anger aimed at her, when I was the one who couldn't play the first damn note?

Then something broke loose. We were making music together, but it was as if the music were a third person standing between us, and all we could do was submit our two voices to the unfamiliar voice of the stranger. I lost my place on the page, and somehow the violin kept playing. For a moment we found ourselves in a village square in Hungary: coal smoke, a crying baby, the hard-baked clay of the square below our feet. It didn't last, of course; couldn't have lasted. My fingers remembered themselves. The music got away. Cynthia had collapsed on the floor, laughing. Her viola and her bow lay untouched beside her.

When the lesson was over, she said, "You know that I've given you that bow, don't you?"

In January, Hannah was back with us during the week. Something had changed about her in the months since school started, or in the way I saw her. All of a sudden, or what seemed sudden from my perspective, having been mostly apart from her those four months, she had come into her own. Her struggles, whatever their nature, no longer had all that much to do with mine.

One night I gave a private concert for Hannah and Cynthia. When they called for an encore, I played "Tennessee Waltz."

"You used to play it better," said Hannah. Thankfully, she was not about to become the steward of her father's happiness.

Cynthia and I lay awake in bed at night and talked music theory: the difference between major and minor thirds. She was having doubts about her musical career, had been having them all along without allowing it to get the better of her. The excitement she saw in me wasn't available to her any more. Now she went between drudgery in the practice room and panic on the concert stage. Her father had been a church organist, and from the time she could hold a quarter-sized fiddle she had been trained as a classical soloist. It never happened, and now, more and more, she was looking forward to another kind of life.

"The most valuable things I learned about music were the things I discovered on my own, outside of the academy. Finding out what the instrument could do, instead of being told."

On a Sunday morning before a rehearsal, she practiced Stravinsky in the living room, cussing under her breath. I wanted to be gone, out of range of her frustration, but it filled the house. She finished a fast passage and blew a raspberry.

"Don't forget to have fun!" I called from the next room.

"I *am* having fun, goddamn it!"

My playing moved from one room to another on a whim. The kitchen had a wooden floor with a full basement under it, which made the violin sound uncharacteristically rich, but I kept returning to the laundry room, my place of secret necessity: the cat in her morning sunlight, the grinning ceramic faces on the patio wall, and that stolid, humorless couple, the washer and dryer. I swiped a framed photograph from the living room and hung it on the wall. A train was climbing a mountain grade somewhere in Mexico, a funnel of dense black smoke streaming from the locomotive. This was the energy I wished to bring to the violin: loud, powerful, dirty, unstoppable.

One Sunday I was practicing Haydn in the kitchen. Cynthia had stayed in bed late, reading. She came into the kitchen wearing her Tweetie bathrobe and looked at me in a way that made me stop in mid-measure.

"Something's missing," she said. "Your technique has really improved, but your expression hasn't caught up with it. It's like you're caught in some deadly struggle."

"You can't save me from it, you know. Struggle is all I've got right now."

After the first of the year she started me on the Vivaldi concerto, which beginning violin students all over the world learn in preparation for their first solo recital. I got stuck on the first line, unable to conceive of playing a lower note on a higher string.

"You learn this sort of thing so you can unlearn it later," she said when she showed me the fingering.

The right notes had always been enough before the Vivaldi. Now she was asking for more— *expression*, she called it. *Depth.* She showed me how a passage might be "interpreted," as if I were capable of something as refined as interpretation, even though we both knew that I wasn't.

"Don't worry about keeping your shifts silent," she said. As a student she had been taught to play the music exactly as it had been written, with no extraneous sound. Now she was determined to teach the opposite and free herself from the tyranny of her training once and for all. "Who cares? Play from your heart, and make all the noise you can."

She wanted me to play the Vivaldi from memory, learning it backwards line by line from the end of the concerto so I wouldn't overlearn the opening movement. She urged me to *press* against the music, to be fully present in each and every note.

"That sounds pretty risky," I said. "What if you put yourself completely into the music and it goes to pieces?"

43

The more she asked for, the less I was able to give. When we were home together, the air in the house thickened with a combustible mixture of hope and fear. Painful experience had taught me that love was not something to be lightly entered into or lightly abandoned. But sooner than I would have chosen or expected, I'd come to a static, unmusical place. The violin had given me a chance to recover from the end of my marriage and my father's death. It's no exaggeration to say that it had saved my life, but it couldn't sustain it; it couldn't bear the weight of my dilemma any more than love could.

We went skiing with Bob, a clarinetist and the director of the community orchestra. He had never turned away anybody who wanted to play with them and came faithfully to rehearsals. At Cynthia's suggestion, he gave me the second violin part for two works they were going to perform in the spring concert, but not the Beethoven; she said I wasn't ready to tackle the spiccando bowings.

Two weeks later I ran into Bob at the post office.

"Are you coming Thursday night?" he said. "First orchestra rehearsal. Have you been practicing?"

"No. I'm still working on the Vivaldi."

"It doesn't matter. Just come."

"But I'm not ready."

"That's not what Cynthia says."

"Cynthia has an unrealistic view of my ability. To say nothing of my commitment."

"You'll never be ready if you don't come. You need to get your feet wet."

"Next year, maybe."

Before every lesson she and I said good-bye, and for the next hour and a half we became teacher and student. When I tried clowning around to break the tension, she was not charmed. The kind of communication that passed between us as man and woman didn't work on lesson night. She required me to communicate with the violin. Once I accidentally put the music on the stand upside down and started to play. For a moment, the clouds parted and we knew each another again as lovers;

then it was back to business. The lessons began to take on the pallor of responsibility. Afterwards, both of us needed to be alone for a while.

At Cynthia's suggestion we went to a concert by the violinist Sergiu Luca, whose performances of Bach's partitas and sonatas for solo violin I had been listening to on tape. More than just a great player, he was a great showman. His bow action was magically light, even when he was digging in. He stood on his toes, or he took a wide stance like a sumo wrestler. The music sucked him upward into the air until he shook himself loose and grabbed hold of the earth once again with his feet. He got so carried away at the end of the Ysaye sonata that he staggered back on his heels and nearly fell.

"That was terrific," I said on the way home. "What I wouldn't give to be able to play like that."

"You should call him before he leaves town and ask for a lesson," said Cynthia.

"You've got to be kidding. Me ask Sergiu Luca for a lesson? He's in a class with people like Perlman and Zucherman."

"You never know. It might be a turning point in your career."

One day she came home from work unexpectedly at noon. I'd been practicing chords. It was already the middle of February, and icicles were melting from the eaves.

"I don't think I can be your student any more," I said before she had a chance to take her coat off.

"That's too bad. I'm not surprised, though. Is it because of me, or Vivaldi?"

"Let's leave Vivaldi out of it. I just need a break."

"From me, or the violin?"

"From the two of you together. I don't want to stop playing. And I don't want to lose you. But I have to find a way to keep you and it separate."

"Funny," she said. "I knew you wouldn't stay with me forever, but I always thought that when the time came, I'd pass you along to another teacher. As if you were mine to give."

I kept working on the first movement until I developed a strawberry on my neck—the badge of a string player. Uninstructed, the concerto finally began to take on a little color and movement, and I was able to learn the whole first movement by heart. Some of the excitement of that morning after my first lesson returned, when I'd walked the streets at sunrise and returned to my dismal apartment to see the bowl of tangelos on the counter—an apparition of life restored.

One movement was enough. Having gone that far, I realized with joy that I never had to play it, or anything else, ever again.

Cynthia and I had one last "lesson" to acknowledge in no uncertain terms that something had ended, but the violin stayed in its case.

"What about your bow?" I said. "It doesn't feel right for me to keep your bow if I'm not going to be your student."

"It's yours. Take care of it. And keep working on your bow action. You'll correct it once you realize that it's holding you back. Your down-bow still looks like you're winding up to throw a fastball."

"What do you think I should work on next?"

"I don't know," she said. "I'm not your teacher any more. The violin is your teacher."

We continued to live together for a couple of months after that, but the stubborn conviction that we had failed each other as student and teacher hung around the house like the smell of old smoke. I practiced the violin when I felt like it, which wasn't very often, and with none of the dedication that had been mine during the year that I had studied with her. Without the common ground of music, she and I no longer came to one another with the same intensity, although it took another year before we could bring ourselves to admit it. After she moved out, the music stand turned into a magazine rack, and the violin hardly made a sound in the closet.

These things happened twenty-two years ago, as I write—not long enough to be safely locked away in a previous, forgotten lifetime, but long enough that they can be remembered with thanks that they are over, and with the affection that is specially reserved for memories of a difficult time. I tried to sell the violin once after Cynthia and I split up, but the money didn't justify the sacrifice. Granted, the instrument isn't doing anybody any good stored away in a closet, and can only go on reminding me of my decision to end what began with such vivid enthusiasm. But it's a useful reminder that, having lived through a difficult time, I'm better prepared to do it again, as my father wrote in his unmailed letter—a prayer, more than a statement of belief, uttered on my behalf from a worthy and loving man. Having lived just short of a lifetime, he might have known a thing or two that I had yet to learn.

Not long ago there was a party at my house. Everyone had gone home but Om Devi and Talissa, who had just discovered that they both played the violin. Having taken it up as adults, they did not pretend that anything would ever come of it besides what it had been from the start— a private pleasure. They stood in my doorway and talked enthusiastically about their instruments.

"I've got a violin, too," I confessed. It was still there on a high shelf in the closet, buried under the camping gear. I put the case on the dining room table in front of my friends and snapped open the lid.

"Oh my God," said Talissa.

The violin bow, Cynthia's present to me those many years ago, had exploded. Horsehair cascaded from either end of it. The velvet lining of the violin case was alive with maggots, wagging in the uncalled-for light of our summer afternoon. I took the violin out of the case and wiped it tenderly with a kitchen towel. At least I'd had enough sense to loosen the strings.

Om Devi said, "You haven't played for a long time, have you?"

Fianchetto

HANNAH, MY DAUGHTER, ASKED ME TO TEACH HER TO PLAY CHESS. She had been teaching school in Istanbul. There, she said, young people take chess lessons the way they take music lessons in the States, but none of her Turkish friends wanted to trouble themselves with a total beginner. This took me by surprise, not so much because she wanted to learn the game, which she had never expressed any interest in before, but because of her sudden forthcomingness. I couldn't remember a time when she had actually come out and asked me to do something with her. She was home for the summer, before leaving for her freshman year at St. John's College, Annapolis. I had not played since high school and no longer even owned a chess set. But yes, of course, I would be happy to teach her.

I learned the game from my grandfather, the Reverend Doctor Thomas Sparks Cline. My mother, his daughter, claimed it was improper to use the "reverend" without the "doctor," as in "Reverend Cline"—a propriety recalled during Princess Diana's funeral service on television, in which the dean of Westminster Abbey and other members of the clergy were called "the reverend doctor" by the British commentator. "Reverend," my mother insisted, was an adjective. It needed something to modify.

When I knew my grandfather, he had retired from the Episcopal ministry. I was too young to have heard him preach in his last church, in Watertown, Connecticut, following assignments in Boston, Philadelphia, and New York. My sisters enjoyed reminding me that I had not yet been born when my grandparents lived in Watertown, so I could not possibly remember anything about it. But I had seen pictures of the church and rectory, and all the famous events of my mother's childhood were set, in my imagining of them, in that tall gray house on the village green.

One of my grandfather's vocal chords had been removed, and he talked in a cheerful, gusty whisper. He was not a pious man. He drank a little scotch, and he never talked about God, at least not in the company of his grandchildren. Our chess games were just games. They never had the stink of instruction. He always beat me, but so amicably that when it was over, I never felt beaten. We played to the death: resigning was not part of the game. He applied the checkmate, laughed, and proclaimed as loudly as he could in his half voice, "Good! Good!"

After my grandmother died, he moved to a home for retired Episcopalian ministers, Druim Moir, outside of Philadelphia. I remember a long, lugubrious building of ivied brick and slate, flowered walks, ponderous furniture, a wainscoted library, old men in black wearing clerical collars, and, except in the kitchen, no women—a monastery, essentially, and overly staid for someone of my grandfather's high, good spirits. Beyond those stubborn convictions in his, our, Protestant lineage that it was neither manly nor godly to complain, it was simply not in his nature. During the first World War, as a young chaplain in France, he wrote letters to my grandmother in Boston that made trench warfare sound like a well-contested game of chess: a struggle, yes, but an interesting one, and bound to end soon. He did not write a word about the suffering of wounded and dying men—only that he regularly gave communion to the troops and exercised the general's horse. Once, with shells exploding nearby, he saw a French officer having dinner in the trench, with a table, a clean tablecloth, and a bottle of wine. This was the view of the war that he sent home to his family.

My grandfather and I almost never saw one another after he moved to Druim Moir, but we began a chess correspondence. He had always been a great writer of letters, gracing his correspondents with pages of florid script. (He had worked his way through college as a scribe.) In letters written to me before I could read, between the lines, he inked little drawings of objects mentioned in the text. His letters, my first knowledge of the written word, intimated that the word "wheelbarrow" and the drawing of the wheelbarrow and the wheelbarrow itself, standing in the garden rows, miraculously partook of the same experience and yet were completely different experiences, each unto itself.

I had days to study each move after we started playing by mail, but taking away the element of time did not bring me any closer to beating him. His postcards brought news of life at Druim Moir: "6. B-K2. Today I planted marigold and cosmos seedlings." He liked to fianchetto his bishops on the knight's second square and so bring strength to bear on the long diagonal. Their latent power was revealed—"discovered," in chess language—when he moved another piece out of the way. In his postcard messages, he never hinted that growing old in a home for widowed Episcopal ministers was anything but a lark.

Hannah met me at the airport when I visited her in Istanbul. She watched while I changed my dollars into millions of Turkish lira and led me through the crowd, past men asking urgent questions, to the minibus. I grew up in New York City, but here I was overwhelmed, clothed in the conspicuousness of the foreigner. This was the first time Hannah had lived in one of the world's great cities. She had only been there a few weeks, but now she was the experienced one. She knew how to say, "I don't speak Turkish" in Turkish. She bought bus tickets for us in the downtown crush. A bus swung around the end of the platform and would have knocked me down had she not grabbed my arm.

For the next two days, the weekend, we saw Istanbul: the gloom of the harem at Topkapi Palace, where the sultan lived under his mother's thumb; the Aya Sofia; the Blue Mosque. On our way into the Aya Sofia a man approached me, presumably to sell something. I lifted my hands—not interested—and kept on walking. He shouted after me: "Never talk to a Turk with your hands!" On the mosque's dark and freezing balcony we saw mosaics of Christian saints that the Moslems had plastered over when they took the city, now being unburied and restored. A Turkish man asked me where we were from, and, innocently—that is, simply curious, rather than seeking some sort of favor—if Hannah and I were married. Greater than the pleasure of hearing that I looked young enough to be her husband was the pleasure of our being seen as peers, equal citizens of the world, rather than parent and child, having already surpassed the hierarchy of knowledge and responsibility that that implies. (She was five the time I fell asleep on the grass at the Albuquerque Zoo, next to the seals, and woke to find her gone. She had wandered off into the snake house. I found her discussing the python with a stranger. "I wasn't lost," she said. "*You* were.")

Hannah shared an apartment on the side of a hill. It had a long balcony and a smoky view of the Bosporus. Asia, they said, lay beyond the murk. Every night at nine, after the last call to prayer, she and her roommates turned off the lights to protest corruption in the Turkish government. Passing cars honked their horns in sympathy. She had not yet turned twenty. I thought: how can anyone so young know anything about corruption? Something had definitely changed in her, and between us, in the time since she had first left home, a high school junior, to study in France. (I'd thrown her my watch across the boarding gate when she was leaving. She needed to make connections, to be securely anchored in a familiar world and time.) Now, as a guest, I was sitting at her dining room table in a foreign city, eating oranges, drinking tea, talking politics, things that neither one of us really knew much about, but talking, nevertheless. It was as if, having put so great a distance between us, we could now be safely interested in each other for the first time.

On Sunday we walked through the dizzying and endless aisles of the Grand Bazaar: meerschaum and amber; camelskin puppets; expensive stone chess sets, the pieces too squat, too much alike one another, and too unlike my grandfather's pieces to be happily playable. I got into an argument with a rug dealer. Americans are capitalists, he said; Turks barter. He gave Hannah the once-over and offered me seven camels for her.

"Twenty," I said.

When the weekend was over, I caught the hydrofoil across the Sea of Marmara for a tour of the Aegean coast. Hannah had to stay in Istanbul and work. I felt like the boy hero in one of those old tales, setting off to meet and overcome dangers. The beginning was always the best part, when he steps forth with nothing but the clothes on his back and the dinner his mother packed for him, when everything familiar is left behind, and anything is still possible, at least until the first monster bars the path. Hannah's Turkish phrase book was my magical talisman. Her goodbye was the blessing of my godfearing parent.

"Queen on her own color," I said when Hannah and I set up the pieces— words first spoken to me when I was seven. My grandfather's board was so vast, really a table with a chess board for a top, that I couldn't reach across into enemy territory without leaving my chair.

We sat in the library of the Buddhist temple where I had lived as caretaker for five years, taking refuge from a second marriage. The temple building and its central chorten had been built in what its Tibetan founders considered an especially auspicious place. A mountain shaped like a turtle to the north, a river to the south, a wide view to the west, and a great rock to the east—a place conducive to ending hostility.

Hannah and I both have the curse of reticence. For years, when she was shuttling back and forth across town between her mother's place and mine, I tried lamely to get her to tell me how things were going. The question was too wide, too abstract. It was too *personal*. It lacked the hook of particularity. Whenever I tried to get her to talk, I sounded frighteningly like somebody's parent.

Now the subject of conversation unfolded on the chess board between us: not her or me, not us, but *it*. We invented a system as we went along: not quite a lesson, and not quite a contest, but a pact—a promise to pay careful attention to the game and to one another. She found her own moves. I questioned and revised. It was nothing like the games I had played with my grandfather, in which the point was loving competition, a way of entering into pleasure with your opponent, but competition, all the same. It would have been against his religion to let me win. Instead, from him I had the kind of motiveless acceptance that a grandparent can give. My success in life, or my lack of it, was not his responsibility. He had no stake in making me into a winner.

Hannah and I played four games over the course of the summer. She won two by checkmate—victories that we engineered together. For once, I had her all to myself. She was not about to leave for her mother's place or to see a friend, nor about to disappear into another foreign country. One night we nodded out and couldn't finish. The game stayed set up in the library for almost two weeks. It drew me in at odd times of the day, eating lunch or sorting through the mail. She had a great combination to play, if only she could see it.

At the end of August she left for college. Her mother and I drove her to the airport, stood in front of the big window, and cried as the plane took off. She had already been leaving home for three years, to France, Israel, Turkey. We should have been used to it.

It would be easy enough to start up a chess correspondence by e-mail. I'm prepared for that to happen or not to happen. Besides the obvious fact that, living away from home and parents, she is more herself than before, is the corollary that her *intellect*—something debased by many of her parents' generation—is likewise coming into its own, and it may bear little resemblance to that of her parents or grandparents. Her latent powers, which up until now have always been colored, if not obscured, by the parental presence and the parental predilection, are just now beginning to be discovered, and those powers are taking forms that, before now, were unimaginable to me.

Last semester I had an e-mail from her: "I'm reading the Meno. We have already torn through Homer and are on to Virtue."

Good! Good!

Love at a Distance

A FEW MONTHS BEFORE THE WORLD TRADE CENTER FELL, my daughter
Hannah moved to New York, of all places—my hometown. Her childhood in New Mexico placed her in the company of those who see what
the boondocks have to offer and leave as soon as they can. I'd made the
opposite move when I was about her age, choosing air, light, and space
over the buzz and rush of the city, and never regretted it. But now and
then—and more often in the years since the attack, with New York and
New Yorkers so rich in the country's affections—I find myself longing for
the city that couldn't keep me.

When the towers fell, Hannah's summer sublet was about to run
out, and she was scouting the city for affordable housing. We admitted
to one another what we might not have admitted in other company, that
it was the ideal time to look for a rental apartment in New York. If people decided that the suddenly extraordinary risks of living there weren't
worth the benefits, and if they decided to go elsewhere, things were sure
to open up, and rents were sure to come down.

One afternoon she called from Dyckman Street, in Inwood—my old
neighborhood. It was famous for Dyckman House, a remnant of Dutch
colonization, where a set of George Washington's wooden teeth were
kept in a glass cage. I gave directions, and when she called again she was
standing across the street from 83 Park Terrace West, where I'd lived
my first eighteen years. It was an odd feeling to have part of me there

again observing the architecture, if you could call it that: a six-story brick apartment house with a fire escape. There on the second floor were the windows that my father cleaned on Sundays after church, when he climbed out on the fire escape with a bottle of Windex and two rags, one to wash and one to dry, while we, his three children, lay sprawled on the living room rug reading the funnies from the *Herald Tribune*. What we saw from inside was the top half of a smiling bald man, apparently suspended in air two floors above the street. When he finished the job, you could see everything better: the nuns on the sidewalk, the tops of cars that had been lucky enough to find a parking place, and on a clear day, New York's sorry excuse for the sky.

I'd left thirty years before my daughter's arrival. Except for one cousin who kept to himself, everyone in my family had long since moved away or died, so for many years there wasn't any reason to visit. I had a New York girlfriend in more recent history, and she and I took turns flying back and forth across the continent. ("Amor de lejos es para pendejos," they say here in New Mexico. Love at a distance is for fools.) She found the Southwest harsh and uncivilized, and I had grown too comfortable with the leisurely pace of life here, which many New Yorkers find infuriatingly slow, to seriously consider moving back east. There were good things about the relationship—the thrill of that first cinematic embrace in LaGuardia after a long separation. She called it "airport joy." We liked missing each other more than being together, and eventually she put an end to it, saying by way of explanation that I didn't want enough for myself. I made halfhearted, rationalizing arguments. I wanted *her*, didn't I? And wasn't knowing what you *didn't* want—for example, living in New York and making a lot of money—a species of ambition?

"It's a good place to raise children," I can imagine my father telling my mother when they first saw our neighborhood in the 1930s. Inwood was the closest thing to nature on the island, with parks on three sides, and a shoreline, and seagulls from a not-too-distant sea—formerly the island's wilderness, as Harlem had been its farmland. The shores of Inwood Park were littered with clamshell middens. Black men in gummy overalls set out eel traps from the rocks on the Manhattan side of Spuyten Duyvil, hurling them into deeper water on the end of a rope. Once caught, the eels were kept alive in a few inches of water at the bottom of a bucket. It was hard to tell one eel from another, or the heads from the tails. I didn't want to touch them.

From the roof of the apartment house you could see the Big Blue C (for Columbia) painted on the sheer rock across the river channel at the Spuyten Duyvil station of the New York Central. Every ten years or so the Big Blue C magically renewed itself. Supposedly the undergraduates repainted it, a difficult undertaking with ropes and hanging scaffolds and barrels of that baby blue paint. My father had gone to Columbia College and then directed the college admissions office, so besides being a fa-mous landmark on the boat tours that circled Manhattan, the Big Blue C was a steadfast reminder of our place in the world. For years, until my father bought season tickets, we watched Columbia football games from the roof, having to guess from crowd noise what had just happened in the near corner of the field, which was hidden by a tree. In one of those dreams that you keep having over and over, I cling to that rooftop, flat on my belly, holding on for dear life as the building sways sickeningly back and forth.

In the street my friends and I played stickball, exciting because of the possibility of broken windows; a game called War in which the names of countries were written on the blacktop with pastel chalk, forming the spokes of a wheel (it was an advantage to be Czechoslovakia because it took longer to say than the names of other countries); and Ringolevio, a complicated and endless game of pursuit, capture, imprisonment, and re-newable freedom that took us into the basement catacombs of the hous-ing projects and got us into trouble with the building superintendent. My Greek hero was an older kid named Johnny Korobos, who could throw a ball all the way from the street onto the roof of his apartment house, though not always on the first try.

A few years ago I was depressed and enrolled in a program designed to help New Mexico state employees in various kinds of trouble. At our first meeting, the therapist—a woman more inclined to offer sympathy, which was what I really needed, than to pry into my past—nevertheless asked where I was from originally. "New York" was not specific enough for her, nor "Manhattan," nor even "Inwood." I told her the address.

"You've got to be kidding," she said. "You lived in 83? I lived in 70, right across the street. Wait. Your father worked for Columbia, didn't he? You had two sisters. One of them went to Music & Art. I knew your family. I knew *you*. You were this skinny little red-haired kid who used to run around in the street with your friends. And do you know what? You are personally responsible for one of the great disappointments of my life. Ever since then, I've always dreamed of having a son with red hair."

The real New York, that is, the one I imagined but had never come to know in the province of Inwood—the New York of extravagant getting and spending, of crowds and traffic and glamorous uproar—lay somewhere to the south. I had glimpses of it growing up, on weekends, when we shopped for school clothes at Gimbel's and Macy's. (My mother: "Are you sure there's enough room in the crotch?") The summer I turned eight, I first took the A train to the West Side YMCA to attend the Summer Adventure Club and, along with the other young adventurers, crossed the black cinder bridle path into Central Park, garnished with the fresh green spoor of horses. In high school, I played pool or walked around the Village with my friend and classmate Eric, a real New Yorker who lived on Central Park West. He ordered falafel from a street vendor with a worldliness that I envied and aspired to, but could never quite bring off. I even ditched classes now and then, rode the subway to Worth Street, and sat in on criminal cases, fascinated by that conjunction of the formal and the pathetic. But I was convinced that I was missing out on the real life of the city, for whatever reasons: because my father, yet another refugee from the boondocks, had taken baths in a horse trough in the hills of West Virginia when he was a boy, or because we were low-church Episcopalians with a dose of Methodism from the southern branch of the family and consequently placed a higher value on "moderation in all things" than on worldly gain or any kind of excitement, including the kind that New York, wherever it was, represented.

Not knowing where else to go after college, I went home. The war in Vietnam was at its worst, and I was draft eligible. My parents didn't seem overly concerned when I spent the summer playing the horses at Aqueduct and Belmont, riding my motorcycle to the track every day to study the *Daily Racing Form* and place $2 bets. I'd won some money for a college essay on characters in the works of Joseph Conrad who are "overwhelmed," in the root sense of the word—tossed over the helm in rough weather. Some swim, others drown, and others, the ones I identified with, float ambiguously between life and death. Dutifully I went to the paddock before each race and checked my horse for "kidney sweat," which a book on handicapping said was a smart thing to do. It was better to lay off a horse with sweaty kidneys. I stayed afloat for nearly three months before losing the last of my fortune at Saratoga Springs.

In California for graduate school, I met Phoebe, a dyed blonde from New York who was studying communications. Her father owned a mattress store in Queens called Foam City. She was smart and beautiful, and we were both a little homesick, and I was drawn to her the way I'm always drawn to New Yorkers when I'm not in New York. We got to communicating, even though she was seeing some preppie named Sumner, and rode around the coastal hills on my motorcycle, she in her studded leather jacket and bell-bottoms, holding tight around my waist, her chin resting dreamily on my shoulder. It took a while for me to confess that she was my first real lover, though she'd probably figured that out on her own, and a while longer for her to reconcile herself to being with an inexperienced man—someone who, while claiming to be from New York, acted more like Nebraska and was not planning to go into medicine, law, or business. Her roommate, who really *was* from Nebraska, warned that if we didn't slow down, we'd use up our allowance of love long before we got married, not that we had any plans yet.

When the draft board caught up with me in San Francisco, I left Phoebe and fled reluctantly, tragically, back to New York, where I took education courses at NYU and, innocent of any practical experience, got a job teaching a fourth-grade class in East Harlem for the draft exemption. On the Bronx side of Spuyten Duyvil I sublet an apartment with a window facing south toward the old neighborhood. The Big Blue C couldn't be seen from there because I was living right on top of it. This allowed me to think I'd escaped its influence. Strange that I'd lived right over there all those years and never once seen *behind* the Big Blue C into the narrow chasm that had been blasted out of rock to lay tracks for the New York Central. Inwood and childhood were now over there, across the water: not gone entirely, but seen from an elevated distance. All of a sudden, with very little encouragement from me, I had the makings of a life: my own place, and a job, and Phoebe, who was still in California. It was all terrifyingly adult.

On the first day of school, one of the other teachers, an ex-Marine with a glass eye that looked through rather than at you, sized me up and said, "These kids will have that long hair of yours out by the roots in nothing flat." In fact, it took them two days to bring me to tears and a week and a half to finish me off. That's when I decided to drive a cab, which didn't take any special talent or resolve. What's more, it would give me something to belong to—New York City, an ocean that I had been tossed into as a newborn without ever getting thoroughly wet. So I tried belonging for a few months, long enough to figure out that driving a cab was hard and dangerous work, requiring quantities of talent and resolve that I didn't have or didn't care to summon. Half a lifetime later, I didn't want to look like Les, one of the cabbies in my garage, who'd already spent thirty years behind the wheel. He carried his teeth around with him in a soap dish. "What are *you* doing here?" he said. "You're a young guy. You got a college education. You ought to be able to get something better."

They made new drivers work Sundays. I learned to pass up the Saturday-night leftovers, who might get sick in the cab, in favor of old ladies on their way to church, shampoo sweet, who usually gave good tips. The rest of the time I worked nights because you could get around town easily. People were in less of a hurry and more likely to tolerate my asking for directions. On my day off, I got up in the middle of the afternoon and walked down by the tracks, under the Henry Hudson Bridge and along the water's edge, and thought about Phoebe, who was planning to come east for a visit. Although we may not have said as much, we needed to decide whether or not to be together, or at least discover if it was too soon, too scary, or too painful to decide.

"You are in love, no?" said a passenger one night, a beautiful Lithuanian woman with a husky voice. I remember her eyes in the rearview mirror. "Be always in love, yes."

Back then it was impossible to anticipate a time when I would be thirty years gone, living far from New York and thinking happily of the time I drove a cab there. It was not a particularly happy time for me, except when I got off work at three a.m. and bought a wreath of figs from the all-night grocer on Jerome Avenue and took another cab home as a passenger. That part—nesting in the back seat of another man's cab after a ten-hour shift and eating figs, with nothing more to do than watch the city slide by—wasn't half bad. The shoes in the display window at Buster Brown were enjoying their hours of privacy, and a little farther down Broadway, you passed through an Elysium of baking smells called Stella d'Oro. The full pleasure of it couldn't have been known to me then, of course, because of things that must have interfered, like how much money I hadn't made that night, or the thought of having to get up and drive again tomorrow, or the pressure to make plans or not make plans with Phoebe. But now I can weed out the uncomfortable things and keep the pleasant ones, the way I ignored the drunks swaying in the middle of the street on Sunday mornings—one hand raised hopelessly, belt high—and sought out the sweet-smelling ladies with their fat purses.

Once I rode home with a cabbie who didn't know my neighborhood. But when we climbed the hill to my apartment, he said, "That's the Spuyten Duyvil station down there, isn't it? I know where I am now. I go fishing down there." I asked if he ever got any eels. "What do you mean, eels? Who'd want to eat one of them things? You can get plenty of stripers if you know how."

Besides the dispatcher at the garage, the only people I talked to were passengers. Everyone else, the friends I would have made if I'd been friendlier, receded into the parallel world of daylight. It was the easy intimacy of strangers that kept me at it, even more than the opportunity to see the essential New York. The person in the back seat and I could safely be ourselves, knowing that the relationship would end in a matter of minutes.

One night I picked up an old babe and drove her crosstown from one bar to another. She was flirting with me on the way over. When she had trouble getting out, I told her how to work the door handle. She gave me a bright, girlish smile from the curb and said, "You know what you just said, honey? You said, 'First you get it in there. Then you grab hold. Then you push and squeeze at the same time.'"

Another time, I was on the way home with my off-duty light on and stopped for a man who was urgently waving me down. He had just lost his cousin in Vietnam. "I called him Sorry Eyes," he said. "When he was going over I said to him, 'Sorry Eyes, don't be a punk, be good to the other guys and don't be afraid to fight.' And you know, the State Department hasn't told us anything yet, but I'll bet on the graves of my three children that he went out like a hero. He was a flame thrower." I took him downtown and we drank whiskey for a while and he cried and talked about his cousin the flame thrower and said one thing for sure, before Sorry Eyes died, he learned what it means to be a man.

Death had moved into the neighborhood. We'd killed our great men—Medgar Evers, the Kennedys, and Martin Luther King, who would have spoken at my college commencement—but it hadn't stopped there. I'd lost a friend in the war, and one of my college roommates seemed headed in the same direction. ("The fat boys fuck up the whole platoon," he wrote from basic training.) Debtors were found floating in Manhasset Bay on a regular basis. Even people like me were susceptible, something I knew but was too young to believe. Besides the Selective Service, every night there was the possibility of picking up the wrong passenger. I contemplated my own loneliness, which was easier to face up to than death, wrote poems, and read difficult books. Every so often I typed out some quotation and taped it to the dashboard next to my hack license. Nietzsche: "Steameth not this city with the fumes of slaughtered spirit?"

Phoebe flew in from California. On her last day in New York, we got up early and dropped acid at my apartment. Between us was the sad understanding that she had to go away again, if only for a while. Even so, or maybe because of it, we had a great day. Aunt Nancy had given me a baked ham for Christmas, and we took snapshots of each other to see if we looked any different when we were high. Phoebe with Ham. Me with Ham. Phoebe and me with Ham (the camera had a shutter timer). I asked permission to spend some time alone with the window, and she said okay. Cars across the river in Manhattan were like drops of water falling horizontally, or like beads on an abacus. They moved because I meant them to. I was convinced that if I raised my finger in a certain way, as I wrote in a journal the next day, "New York would fall in ruins."

We became verbal again in late afternoon, and practical matters began to assert themselves. What were we going to have for dinner? Certainly not our chaperone, the ham. Meanwhile, what were we going to do with our lives? The most important thing, we decided, was for us to be together. We both loved New York, at least we did that afternoon. But we really wanted to live someplace warm like California where you could ride a motorcycle year round.

When I drove Phoebe to the airport the next day, the New York skyline looked more beautiful than ever, or beautiful for the first time, because I'd made up my mind to leave as soon as possible. To this day I've never been inside the Chrysler Building, but my eye always goes to it first, whether the building itself or a picture of it, what with those lovely arches stepping up and up, like a giant jukebox, and the knowl-edge that my mother had worked there as a secretary, way up at the top, before she married my father. She could feel the building bend in the wind as her fingers breezed over the keyboard at seventy words per min-ute. Skyscrapers, she explained to her children, were designed to bend so they wouldn't break.

At Kennedy, Phoebe took snapshots of the TWA terminal until the shutter jammed. She bought the *Times*, and some Good & Plenty to eat on the plane. Then we held each other like Bogart and Bacall, right in front of all the other passengers.

One of my last nights on the job, late in December 1969, I parked the cab downtown and went to a lecture by Jorge Luis Borges. He talked about losing his sight. It had happened gradually over a period of years, and he did not feel sad or bitter about it, he said, because it had given him the privilege of seeing things in a new way. Time flowed more slowly, as down a gentle slope. The faces of friends were lost, the look of a certain street corner in Buenos Aires, the words on the pages of his books, but in their place, he had the memory of them, which was something different. Then he read that poem about being in Buenos Aires and missing Cambridge, Massachusetts, where he'd lived for a while: it wasn't so much Cambridge that he missed, but the memory of being there and missing Buenos Aires.

These days I entertain similar feelings for New York—a nice place to visit, certainly, but also a nice place to be born and leave behind and remember with a bittersweet tang of longing, the way one remembers a love affair that might have happened but never met its promise.

Hannah found a very small apartment in Harlem, a part of New York that I had seen only from a distance as a child, whenever we drove down Harlem River Drive in my father's car, and later for the ten days I taught school there. "The slum," my father called it—another whole city of dreary buildings and poor people. White people didn't go to Harlem then, much less live there. But in 2001 the neighborhood just north of Central Park was changing, and certain streets, Hannah's among them, were considered safer than others. Besides, New York was a much friendlier place after September 11 than it had been: the attack by a foreign enemy had made New Yorkers more likely to see through the differences between them, and for a while, at least, the city enjoyed a spirit of common destiny and unreserved good will toward just about everyone. A flower importer had donated tens of thousands of daffodil bulbs to the city in memory of those who had died, and when I visited Hannah the following spring, Central Park was a paradise of yellow blossoms. New Yorkers of every kind came out of their apartments to celebrate spring and the fact of being alive; I'd never seen so many smiling people on the streets of that city. A teenager was cutting daffodils in the park—

was he going to take them home to his mother, or sell them? Never mind. The city was his, now, not mine.

The street outside of Hannah's apartment was never quiet at night, which had the same effect on me as sleeping next to a river in the Rockies, a constant murmur of police sirens, domestic fights, garbage trucks, and excited conversation—an all-night-long commotion that could be counted on never to stop and so induced delicious sleep. Hannah had found her way to the exuberant, pulsing heart of New York City, as different from the river junction in the hills of northern New Mexico where she had started life as it could be. Without much conscious intention beyond the need to find an affordable place to live, she had been led into the interior city that I had wanted so much to know when I was on my own for the first time, driving a cab at night and returning before dawn to the sublet on the hill above Spuyten Duyvil, where you couldn't hear anything at night but the air conditioner, and the Big Blue C—the banner of my father's escape from the farm and making good in the halls of education and commerce—worked its domesticating influence on me as I slept.

"I don't care about quality," Phoebe had said when we went shopping for a diamond engagement ring on 47th Street, "as long as it's big." But I was too young and too uncertain about everything to get married. When it was over between us—after she took the ring off her finger, tied it into a shamrock-green bandana, wordlessly handed it back to me, and left me alone in my apartment in the Bronx—what became of her? Did she marry a lawyer and live soberly as a wife and mother in suburban New Jersey? Whatever became of those plans we'd made in the aftermath of our world-shaking acid trip to live on nothing more than air and poetry and love, if it came to that?

Saturday morning. Hannah and I walked uptown through Harlem along Adam Clayton Powell, Jr., Boulevard, which had still been Seventh Avenue when I was a cabbie.

"I've never been here before," I said in wonder. "I grew up in New York and not once until now have I ever walked on this street."

But I had seen it from a distance, under circumstances long forgotten. On the hill above Powell Boulevard, we could see the back side of the Cathedral of St. John the Divine, in the neighborhood called Morningside Heights. That hill marks the abrupt western boundary of Harlem. My great aunt Nor (short for Eleanor, my mother's mother's sister) and her husband George had lived in an apartment off Morningside Drive, where we visited them over the years, drank sherry in their sunless living room (there was never anything to eat along with the sherry), and listened to them bicker like the Smallweeds in Charles Dickens's novel *Bleak House*. From their balcony, wide enough to set out potted plants, you could just see Seventh Avenue far below and the bottomland between it and the East River—Harlem, drowning in a swamp of blue smoke. George had retired from his job as bursar at the Cathedral of St. John the Divine when, one afternoon, two men somehow made their way into the apartment, tied them up, and took what they could find.

In his old age, George never tired of telling the story and bragging about what he would have done to those two sonsofbitches if he'd had a gun. The event went down in family history as a reminder of what a dangerous world it was—how thin-skinned the illusion of safety that our place in the urban landscape afforded us. The slum dwellers could not be trusted to stay in their place in the bottom, but were likely to rise up without warning, tie our hands, and run off with our possessions. We, the children, were allowed to understand that what those men had done was against the law, and that George, who became a pitiful old man because of it, was to be forgiven the homicidal fantasy that nagged him for the rest of his days.

It's easy to feel charitable toward poor folks from a safe remove, something Dickens called "telescopic philanthropy." It's harder to conjure up feelings of compassion when thieves and murderers confront you in the flesh. Not long after September 11, at a previously scheduled event, the Vietnamese monk Thich Nat Hanh spoke to a large crowd at the Cathedral of St. John the Divine, where my uncle George had balanced the books all those years. Thich Nat Hanh asked the crowd to imagine the suffering of the people who'd carried out the attack on the World Trade Center and the Pentagon. Their suffering must have been very great, he said, to have done what they had done. For me, listening to a recording of the talk, it was the sanest response to the attack that I'd heard amid the chorus of panicky, vengeful, and hindsightful voices coming over the airwaves. But two months later, when my daughter was attacked in the lobby of her apartment house in Harlem, beaten unconscious, and robbed of a dozen eggs, my compassion for her attacker failed to come forward.

At the end of our Saturday morning walk up Powell Boulevard, we got on the subway at 125th Street. The summers that I'd taken the A train downtown from Inwood to the Summer Adventure Club, 125th was the last stop before the long, fast ride to 59th. It was my secret joy to stand at the window in front of the first car with my hands cupped on either side of my eyes to shut out the reflection of the subway car behind me, all those dour people on their way to work, and pretend that I was flying in a trackless outer space. The man driving the train, invisible in his man-sized metal box just to the right, had no idea that he had been relieved of his command.

We got off at 207th, the last stop on the line, and climbed the stairs to the street. The sight of it made me dizzy. Nothing had changed in the thirty plus years since I'd last stood on that corner. The people were mostly first- and second-generation Dominicans, where before they had been the sons and grandsons, daughters and granddaughters of Europeans, but the neighborhood was still the neighborhood, and I knew it all immediately, right down to the cracks in the sidewalk. Hannah made motions to go on. I just wanted to stand and look. It was more than I could take in at the speed of walking. Everything asked to be remembered. The corner candy store was no longer the candy store, and yet somehow *it was*. In essence it had not changed since my earliest experience of trading money for goods: bubblegum cards and yoyos, wax lips and peashooters. They still sold newspapers and comic books; they still sold milk in quarts, although plastic jugs had replaced paper cartons.

Up through Inwood Hill Park—the scenic route. It had not been improved and did not need improving: green grass and dandelions, the same old people on the same old benches, mothers walking their own babies, whereas downtown they walked the babies of people whose families had arrived in New York long ago. Hannah kept checking on me: she wanted to be sure that it all wasn't too much, but more than that, she wanted to see New York the way I was seeing it—in perspective. She had her own childhood place to remember in New Mexico, and she resented that the subsequent owners of that river junction had gone and made it better, that it would never be the same place again in the way that Inwood had become the same place for me.

At the top of the hill, Park Terrace West had not progressed much, either. If anything, it was cleaner, but it was impossible to approach it with other than exaggerated praise. At once it was what it was and what it had been, invested with a depth of time that, as likely as not, I alone among its present-day inhabitants could give it. At 83 Park Terrace West, Hannah waited patiently while I read the names on the list in the lobby. Incredibly, there was one that I recognized: LUST.

Something was wrong, but it took a moment to actually *see* it, since it had never been there before, and another moment to name it. That curving gray monolith down at the end of the block, where Park Terrace West meets 218th Street, didn't belong: they had replaced the wooden stadium at Baker Field, where we doggedly watched Columbia lose football games week after week, year after year, with one made of concrete. We walked down the hill, sat in the new stadium with a fairly good crowd attending a track meet, and watched as seven sinewy women ran the 880 on a cinder track circling the field.

I still knew the old Columbia fight songs: "Oh, Who Owns New York?" and "Roar, Lion, Roar." And the beautiful, stately alma mater: "What if the morrow bring sorrow or anything other than joy?" Hannah thanked me for not singing.

Capitalism

THE GOOD HOTEL WAS FULL. Our room at the MGM was tiny, but it had its own toilet, curtains, a radio, and one twin bed. Trams roared past on the street below—deafening, apocalyptic beasts spitting showers of blue sparks that lit up the walls of our room like summer lightning. I loved the hellish, monstrous rush of the trams and the drama of being in a crummy hotel room in a foreign capital with my Polish lover.

Elena blamed Poland for her thinness. Life in her country was not worth living, she said, and it had only gotten worse since the downfall of the Soviets. Even when you could get food, it was hard to get interested in eating it.

Warsaw was bitterly cold. Patches of filthy snow lay in the shadows. The cars, mostly Polish Fiats, were caked with a black sludge up to the door handles, the fallout from coal fires. She said it would be warmer in her city, Poznan. We clung to one another in the brutal cold and made our way through the crowds to the station. A man with a stutter stopped us and explained at great length that he was not from Warsaw, that he had come to the city to visit and had all his things stolen and had no way of getting home. Elena gave him some money even though she did not believe his story. When one of the notes blew out of her hand I chased it desperately across the cobblestones. One hundred złotys— about one cent.

If there were other people in our compartment on the train to Poznan, I do not remember them. Hot air poured from under the seat. We had been cold for two days in Warsaw, all except the time we spent in bed at the MGM. In and out of sleep, I was conscious of seeing us as a third person, another traveler, might have seen us: the lovers, no longer young, not much wiser for loves of the past, recently reunited after a long separation, still in the earliest, blissful hours of their time together, the woman miraculously supporting her head against the man's chest, her hand clutching his shoulder like a fruit bat, the two breathing in and out together, a single satisfied organism. We were in love in the furious, exclusive way that creates privacy in a crowd, even while rubbing elbows and knees with strangers. Before long, doubt about the future was sure to come. But we were still too close to the moment of being back together—Elena rushing at me *all at once* out of the crowd in the airport (wasn't it odd and terrifying how somebody could be entirely missing from your life one moment and entirely occupy it the next, with no degrees of absence or togetherness in between?)—to admit thoughts of the outcome, what would happen after I left Poland. The possibilities had been taking shape ever since the last time we were together. Friends had been predicting two kinds of catastrophe: What if it didn't work out? What if it did? The future seemed impossibly distant in the paradise of our train compartment, although it would not be true to say it did not vaguely exist. What power could our intentions have over us, whether to be together or to be apart? We were together already, and warm, at least for the moment.

Traveling west through Wielki Polska—Big Poland—we passed frozen places with only a few feeble electric lights to show that there was something there, and then the thick of night again. Every so often I would open my eyes, look out at the black countryside, the shapes of junked machinery in a greasy railway yard, and congratulate myself on being on a night train in a foreign country with a foreign woman.

"It's too dark," I said. "I can't see anything."

"There's nothing to see."

"I want to see it anyway. Are there any cows?"

"Of course." She opened her eyes and gave me a fierce foreign look. "Do you think that only Americans have cows?"

"You mean if it was daylight I could see cows?"

"No. They're inside, waiting for spring."

I saw a man holding a kerosene lantern on a station platform. Even in the dark he looked dirty.

My dreams in Poland had to do with helpless sinking into some unsupporting and suffocating substance, usually snow. I sink down through the snow for an unreasonable length of time before coming to rest at the bottom, on my back, so that I am looking up, through the tunnel made by my sinking body, toward what little is left of the world's light. It is useless to struggle, which would only make things worse.

It was not yet daylight. Elena was asleep beside me; her two children, Marek and Dorote, were asleep on the floor. The whole apartment had been turned into a bed for the night; there was no other place to be except in bed. The light in the fish tank stayed on during the night, and the word RYBY ("fish"), each letter cut from a magazine, was taped to the front of the tank. A catfish lashed out in a fury across the tank, stirring up clouds of fish turds and terrorizing the guppies. Elena was in love with this one—the Monster, she called it. When it fastened its mouth against the inner surface of the glass, she kissed it, called it husband, and whispered endearments in her native tongue.

When daylight entered the room through the curtains, she cast her leg across my body, hauling me back to the surface from my dreams of lonely descent, and in this way, more or less asleep, we took inventory of each other's bodies. The light grew and filled the room, touched us and the sleeping children. One crow called from a distance, then more crows, conversing. Then the doves started, in phrases of three notes, like the doves back home.

"Doves," I said.

"Co mówisz?" And then, waking, "What did you say?"

"Ptaki. Can you hear them?"

"Golebi. I love this sound. How do you say it in English?"

"Dove."

I wrote the word on her ovulation chart and, until I left Poland, read it every morning when writing down her temperature.

Andrzej wore very thick glasses, talked a lot, drove very fast, and smoked all the time. His Polish had that heavily stressed, pleading, earnest intonation that gives an impression of deep conviction, even when telling you that his clutch was going out. The car was the kind everybody drove, a Polish Fiat, orange, five years old and falling apart. He was sitting on one of those car seats made of strung wooden beads, a sign of encroaching Western decadence. He grinned at me from behind the glasses and offered me a Marlboro. I grabbed the dashboard when he turned a corner, reminded myself to keep breathing, and, unable to follow his conversation with Elena, who was sitting in back, looked out at nighttime Poznan and thought about dying.

They were talking business. Andrzej was starting a bookstore, and Elena was going in with him. They had to act fast because a box stall had come up for sale in one of the newer housing projects in Poznan, the beginnings of a homemade shopping mall on the ground floor of one of the apartment buildings. Thousands of people lived in the housing project. It was a great opportunity. Andrzej wanted to carry a little of everything, Mickey Mouse and Nietzsche, dirty magazines, a Polish translation of the *Bhaghavagita*. If both of them put in all the money they had, they could buy the box stall and enough books to get started.

While she and Andrzej carried on about the price of the box and how much they might get its owner to come down, her hand secretly reached around the seat and found mine. She had wanted to sit in the back and make out, but I insisted on sitting in front. "Andrzej isn't the chauffeur, you know," I said, not wanting to be too odiously American right at the start.

I liked Andrzej, the way he smiled unsuspiciously at me, the skill with which he kept the Fiat on the road when, trying to light one cigarette from another, hot ash dropped between his legs and smoldered briefly among the bourgeois wooden beads. My opinion was valued and solicited because I was American and therefore an expert on running a business.

"Run it like a newsstand," I said. "Don't try to carry too many titles at first, just the popular stuff you know people will buy. Then later on you can expand."

The Communists had built acres and acres of featureless twelve-story apartment buildings and parking lots and planted a few malnourished trees among them. The housing projects smelled of too much humanity squeezed together in too little space. These were the *new* projects, and the memory of newness had not yet worn completely off. If you needed a place to live, you would consider yourself lucky to get one of these apartments, which still carried a degree of prestige and the tenor of progress.

Shops were being set up in a single, ground-level lobby with a bare concrete floor, greenish overhead fluorescent lighting, and not much heat. Disco music with an industrial beat was piped in ceaselessly. People in overcoats were working late to prepare for the grand opening in a few days, cutting up plywood and hauling in merchandise. The boxes were freshly painted in high-gloss brown and white enamel. The front of each box was a plywood lid that took two people to open and prop up with galvanized water pipes so you could lock up your wares at any time, even when the mall was open during the day.

Capitalism was really very simple. All you had to do was find a place to set up shop, buy some things to sell at a higher price than you paid—it didn't really matter what kinds of things—then you just sat there and got rich. I suggested to Elena and Andrzej that people ordinarily like to handle books before buying them, so they might want to put out some copies on the counter.

Most of the shop owners were going to sell packaged food items, something new in Poland, where food used to sit naked on the shelves or in bins, saving waste and showing you exactly what you were getting. But no, we were talking free enterprise now. There was a sausage concession; a meticulously organized men's store, each shirt wrapped individually in clear plastic; and a place to buy oil and air filters, widely but evenly spaced on the shelves.

A tall, mustached man, the manager, shook hands powerfully with Andrzej and me and kissed Elena's hand. He led us through a corridor with storage lockers on either side (they had big doors and heavy handles, like jail cells or walk-in coolers) to a small office at the rear. The current owner of the box was a woman, darkly dressed, friendly, someone apparently at ease in matters of money, someone whose hand the manager did not kiss. After introductions, a sufficient number of chairs were dragged in from across the hall, and everybody except Elena and me lit cigarettes, including two men who shared the office with the manager and were contributing their share of smoke to the businesslike atmosphere. After some talk, Andrzej pulled out a wad of bills three inches thick. The money was counted, papers signed, figures recorded in ledgers, cigarettes mashed out. On the way out, I grinned at the manager as he gave me another bone-splintering handshake.

It was after eleven by the time Elena and Andrzej finished inspecting their box, opening and closing the plywood lid many more times than necessary to establish that it did, in fact, open and close, and discussing how they would set things up. Everybody else had gone home after applying padlocks to both ends of their box and pasting inch-wide strips of newsprint across the closed lids, so they could not be opened without tearing the paper. That way, if someone broke into the box during the night and stole the merchandise, the newspaper would be torn and you would know for sure that you had been robbed.

Fog had moved over the city. It freshened the air with the smell of seawater and drowned the street lamps. By the time we found our way back to the Fiat, the euphoria of owning a business was starting to wear off. Elena sniped at Andrzej for accepting the asking price for the box, without talking the woman down. Andrzej didn't want to hear about it. Then the Fiat wouldn't start. What the business really needed, said Elena, was a better car, one they could depend on for hauling books to the store. Andrzej said something to the effect that Elena didn't know her ass from a hole in the ground when it came to cars *or* business.

The car started. Elena and I sat in the back while Andrzej drove, pounding the steering wheel and delivering speeches to the rearview mirror, his eyes, behind the glasses, shrunken to angry peepholes.

Andrzej came day and night to Elena's apartment to talk. The two of them stood and argued for hours—Elena was at least as long-winded, loud, and vociferous as Andrzej—while I read or washed the dishes and pretended not to be there. Andrzej smoked punishingly and paced back in forth in front of the windows, from which we could see another apartment block, identical and parallel to ours, and the courtyard in between where people walked their dogs, beat their rugs, watched their children play, and hung out their laundry. The windows were dirty, and Elena promised to wash them before Easter to keep from disgracing the family. Most of the time she took pains to keep the windows closed and the curtains drawn so the neighbors could not spy on us. ("If these women see you with your shirt off," she told me, "tomorrow they will be washing the windows in their brassieres, and the old ones will be sitting behind their curtains masturbating like crazy.") But the window on the left, sometimes used for communicating with Marek and Dorote in the courtyard, stayed open when Andrzej was there to let the smoke out.

The most sense I could make of these discussions was that Elena, having invested her life's savings, about fifteen hundred dollars, wanted to have a say in how things would be run, and Andrzej, who claimed to know a thing or two already about the retail book trade, wanted to manage things by himself. He could not accept the compromise of power that went along with having an equal partner. But if he didn't need her advice, why did he keep coming over?

One night, Elena, Dorote, Marek, and I all fell asleep on the grown-up bed. The television stayed on and nobody had the energy to get up and turn it off. I could hear the voices of American actors submerged beneath the Polish translation. One male actor dubbed all the parts, male and female, all equally without expression.

Andrzej found us there about ten and took Elena away to sign some papers.

"I will tell you about it tomorrow," she said on her way out. "It is like some kind of crazy story."

Instead of going back to sleep, I made tea and sat on the stool in the kitchen, watching people getting ready for bed across the courtyard. It was raining a little. The window was tilted open. I could hear traffic on the wet pavement of Swoboda (Freedom Street), a lovesick cat, the voices of people walking through the courtyard in the dark. Nothing, not even Elena, could make me want to live in this country, which I perceived as the final chapter of human civilization, what was left after industry had ravaged the landscape, darkened the sky, and fouled the water. Never mind. Spring was coming, and grass was starting to show in the sad patches of earth along the walks.

Across the courtyard, a single color television stayed on. Everybody else had gone to bed. My feet rested on a heap of potatoes and onions under the counter. They felt good against the bare soles of my feet, and I thought of the Polish earth they had come from and which clung to them still, warm days to come, cucumbers and tomatoes.

Someone had spilled a gallon of white paint in the parking lot where Andrzej and I unloaded the boxes of new books. The paint was still wet, so we had to step over it on every trip. We carried the boxes through the storeroom, the long, tomblike corridor, and set them on the floor of the stall. It was almost dark. The books still had to be shelved and priced that night because the mall was going to open for the first time in the morning, and Andrzej wanted to be ready.

Almost everyone had left by the time we got there. The stalls were closed, locked, and sealed with strips of newspaper. Two women in green aprons, their heads wrapped in kerchiefs, were mopping the floor, and the couple in the next box were stocking their shelves. They were very organized. The man took the shirts out of the boxes, placed them on the counter for his wife to shelve, and broke the empty carton down with a startling smack of his fist. Then he made a neat pile of the collapsed boxes in the aisle.

Andrzej paced, smoked one cigarette after another, drank a can of beer. He was thinking about business. I was cold. I wanted to get done, go home, and crawl into bed with my ninety-eight-point-six-degree Polish woman.

"One moment," said Andrzej in English, and disappeared into the back.

I lay down to wait on one of the benches in the sales area, which had been built over a reptilian radiator that may or not have been working. When I woke up, the manager, the man who had kissed Elena's hand, was standing over me, and the two cleaning ladies were standing timidly behind him. I sat up quickly.

"Czy pan czeka Andrzeja?" asked the manager. Are you waiting for Andrzej?

"Tak," I replied. "Czekam." Yes. I am waiting.

Andrzej's car was seriously broken down, and nobody was minding the store. The starter needed to be repaired, and he had taken a taxi downtown to find parts. I, Elena, Andrzej's roommate, and another friend of Andrzej's, a mechanic who had been working on the Fiat that morning, sat in the living room drinking coffee and tea. The two men were smoking. A color television was tuned to an old Polish film, a historical drama of the Polish monarchy. Guys in long hair and flared shirtcuffs were bending iron bars to show how strong they were.

Elena and the roommate were talking about cars. Elena wanted to buy a car, even though she did not know how to drive, so she could commute to the bookstore and help with the business. When she spoke, the two men listened with exaggerated attention.

It was raining. In Poland, the days of rain were the clearest days because the rain pulled the pollution down out of the atmosphere. You actually could see farther when it was raining than when it wasn't. The mechanic lit a cigarette. Not being able to converse, I watched the others and smiled when they said something funny.

Andrzej returned, crestfallen. He had not been able to find the parts he needed and had to buy a whole new starter from a Russian on the street. It had cost half a million, and he wasn't even sure if it was the right one.

In the rain, I could almost see distant trees; I could almost breathe. Andrzej stood there smoking up a storm, telling us what had happened. He held the starter in the crook of his arm like a football. His hands were black from working on the car. Elena and Andrzej went into his bedroom to talk about money. The mechanic had gone back out in the rain to install the new starter, so now it was just me and the roommate and the fellows on the television in their frilly shirts. The hero was bending the bars of his jail cell into pretzels. The starter was the wrong one, and when Andrzej went to get his money back, the Russian was gone.

That night, Andrzej came over to talk. Elena put on a bathrobe and they shut themselves in the kitchen for over an hour, at first raising their voices, then speaking less and less, until the pauses in between speeches became very long. Finally, Andrzej came out, looked at me, shrugged his shoulders, and left. He wanted to pay her back what she had paid for the books and the stall and take over the business. She wanted to kill him.

As Holy Week approached, the neighbors dragged rugs down the stairs from their apartments and across the courtyard to a shallow pit at one end—the rug-beating stadium. There the rug was hung from a length of pipe worn as smooth and shiny as a handrail in a train station. They beat their rugs with brooms and hockey sticks and tree branches. The sound of rugs being beaten rocketed off the walls of the tenement, kept us awake at night, and woke us first thing in the morning.

One afternoon a squad of women and girls appeared in the court-yard carrying rakes. The women wore aprons, and their heads were wrapped in towels. They picked up all the trash and carried it away in plastic sacks, and what was too small to be picked up was raked into piles with the dead grass and burned. They raked every inch of the courtyard, so that for days after, you could see the scratches their rakes had made on the ground.

Other women came with enormous bundles of wet laundry tied up in bedsheets and strung clothesline from a pentagon of steel posts in the courtyard, which boys sometimes used for soccer goalposts. Everywhere, curtains were drawn apart—first the heavy winter curtains, which kept out the cold, then the gauzy white summer curtains, like bridal veils, starchy to the touch. Windows opened that had not been opened all winter, and people cried out when they saw their friends in windows across the courtyard, as if they had not seen them in all that time. Those with rugs that still needed cleaning stayed out long after dark, and in the last few days before Holy Week, the pace of the beating became urgent. The sound of rugs being beaten in our courtyard and in neighboring courtyards, throughout the tenements, was like gunfire.

We put off cleaning until the night before Palm Sunday, nearly bed-time, when Elena announced, "The windows are dirty. Tomorrow is a special day. My mother will not be happy if I wait until tomorrow to wash the windows."

"Let's forget it," I said. "Who else is going to notice?"

"No, we cannot forget it. If everybody helps, it will not take very long."

She prepared one bucket of soapy water and one with vinegar in it, and all four of us pitched in. Because I had the longest arms, Elena asked me to wash the outsides, so I held on to the window frame with one hand and swung out into the young evening: smells of thawing earth, laundry, garbage.

The rug beating stopped at midnight. Three hours earlier, I had been ready to sleep, but now I lay wide awake in bed, watching the Telkom Teletra sign flash red, white, and blue through the immaculate window glass.

Elena came back from her meeting with Andrzej smelling even more strongly than usual of cigarette smoke. He had brought a lawyer with him this time. After some hours they had reached a tentative agreement whereby Elena would sell the box to Andrzej and receive her share of any profit on the sale of the books she had helped buy. But when Andrzej was driving her home he changed his mind. The deal was off.

Next morning she woke up with a headache and said she was going to get her own lawyer. The children were fighting. I burrowed under the covers.

"Poor Tom," said Elena.

"Poor Tom," said Dorote. "Always poor Tom. What about me?"

April, the Poles say, is like weaving winter and spring together into a basket. To help ourselves forget that time was passing, we invented tasks. Go to the post office and call Jacek, the children's father, to get some child support money. Buy another loaf of bread. Find some used furniture and fix up the apartment to make life a little less difficult.

The furniture store stood at the end of a dirt lane. Fruit trees were blossoming, the lilacs were beginning to leaf out, and flowers grew in postage-stamp gardens. Someday, said Elena, she would like to have a little house of her own, a yard, a garden—nothing much, just a little space, freedom from worry, a place to sit and watch things come up out of the ground.

The furniture was depressing. We huddled together on a bench waiting for the bus home.

"Life in this apartment is slowly killing me," she said. "Do you think there might be some kind of poison in the walls?"

A gray bird with a black head was walking on the grass. It had a mate. You could tell they were married from the way they walked, apparently ignoring each other, but getting just so far and no farther apart, always circling slowly back to the center of the foraging radius.

"Some birds mate for life," I said.

"I hate not to know what will happen to me and my children. If I cannot get a visa to the U.S., I do not want to live in Poland. Maybe I will go to Norway and find a husband." She pulled my arm tightly around her. "But it will be hard to get used to kissing anybody but you."

Elena, Dorote, and I washed our faces, put on clean clothes, took our passports, and rode a tram to the United States embassy. Three motionless bodies, sleeping or dead, were stretched out on the grass near the railroad tracks.

At the embassy gate, they stuck a metal detector in Elena's handbag and found her pocketknife. It would be held for her until we were finished. As always, there was a long line to apply for visas. A woman held our place while we sat in the warm sunshine, in the park on Ulica Frederyka Chopina. Elena wove a flower braid for Dorote, and she wore it on her ankle.

After an hour we went back to stand in line at the embassy. A teenage girl came out of the building in tears, consoled by an older man. An old woman suffered a heart attack while talking to the consul and was taken away in an ambulance.

The consul was young, a bearded American with long hair tied in a pony tail. He and the others sat behind a glass partition. He asked Elena why she had overstayed her visa when she was in the United States. It was obvious from the tone of their voices that things were not going well. At one point the consul asked, "Where is your home?" "My home is where I am," she fired back at him. They were still arguing at four o'clock, after everybody else in the office had gone. At last he handed her passport back, saying she had not given him sufficient reason to believe that if the visa were granted, she would ever return to Poland. She claimed her pocketknife at the gate and did not speak on the way home.

After dark, we walked north of the apartment block. Trees were blooming in people's yards. It was the first warm evening of the year.

"What right does one person have to tell another where they can be or cannot be?" she asked. "They have all the power and they use this power against people. They say they are there to help but they do not really want to help. They only want to help themselves to keep the power."

"We could always get married," I said. "Even the word scares me half to death."

She laughed. "Our love is like a cake. We are eating it. It tastes very sweet, but all time we are thinking what will we do when the cake is gone. This kind of a cake will make us sick."

"I need some time," I said.

"How much time do you need?"

"Three months."

"Three months? This is too long. Do you expect me to wait three months? I will be in Norway working while you are making up your mind."

On my next to last day in Poznan, we lay down for a nap in the afternoon. Elena dreamed that I was with another woman, someone I had known before her. In the dream she confronted me with it, but I didn't seem to care.

"I did not know you could be this way," she said when we were awake. "Why do you say nothing? Why don't you tell me that this cannot happen?"

At the train station I changed my remaining złotys back into dollars. We said goodbye for a long time, then it was time to go. Just as the train to Warsaw was pulling out of the station, there was a flash and a single clap of equinoctial thunder. Spring had finally come, now that I was leaving. From the train I saw single-horse plows, fields of new wheat, hops vines, a boy herding a sow and two piglets, an old man swinging a scythe, a woman who had ridden her bicycle into the field to hoe, the orange sun going down. A man showed me some wilted roses, but I didn't want to buy them.

Soledad

for Robert Seigen Yosan Winson

WITH PLENTY OF TIME TO KILL AT THE AIRPORT in Mexico City, I sat on a bench in front of a Chivas Regal ad—a picture of a top-heavy blonde holding a croquet mallet over one shoulder, bent over with laughter.

"La vida es para vivirla," said the ad. Life is for living. Robert had known this; more than that, he'd embodied it. Certainly he struggled, like everyone, to live the way he wanted; but I'd never known anyone who was quite so adept at doing it without regret.

I'd met him at the temple some years before he was ordained as a Zen priest. A gnome in faded layman's robes and a forked beard approached me in the courtyard after Sunday lecture and quoted Lewis Carroll's Caterpillar.

"Who are *you?*"

"I hardly know, sir, just at present."

We were friends from then on; surely would have been friends forever. For years, almost until he went into the hospital, we met regularly at our café to talk about "the Zen industry," literature, and love. When my marriage was in trouble—practically all of the time—he listened with faithful interest.

"Why does it hurt so much?" I asked him when things were looking especially bleak.

"Simple. Because you're alive."

Now he'd gone beyond suffering, leaving the rest of us behind to make the best we could of this same-old incarnation.

The Rancho San Felipe had no street address. Originally built as a residence for the archbishop of Oaxaca, it later became the governor's *casa chica*, where he stayed with his mistress and second family. His heirs had broken it up into apartments, but only one daughter, "the Señorita," still lived there, in a house some distance from the other buildings, down a lane flanked by eucalyptus trees.

Naomi, the Rancho's de facto social director and historian, said that in the old days, a newcomer like me would have been formally introduced to the Señorita on my arrival, but such formalities were rarely observed any more.

"The Señorita could have had any man she wanted," said Naomi. "She was beautiful and rich. Lots of men wanted her, but her brothers terrorized them. Nobody was good enough. She had lovers, of course, but the brothers were protecting their own interests. They chose to believe that all of the boyfriends were just after her money, and after a while they just stopped trying. She lives all by herself in that huge house."

My apartment, sublet from a woman who imported folk art to the States, was decorated with curiosities: a colonial sword hung precariously over the front door, threatening to fall with the next earth tremor; many vases with dusty paper flowers; and the indigenous images of death one finds everywhere in Oaxaca, a priest skeleton saying his rosary; a fisherman skeleton casting his net; a pair of bride and groom skeletons, their heads trembling on spring necks, she with a scrap of surgical gauze over her face, grimly holding her bridal bouquet. Robert would have loved it.

The bathroom was overrun with large, translucent ants that drowned in the toilet bowl, although not often enough. I made an ant trap out of a jar lid filled with honey. Rosita, the maid, laughed at it. "Para las hormigas no hay otro remedio. Veneno, entiende? Espray. R-r-r-aid."

For two weeks I spoke to no one besides Naomi and Rosita. I imagined the Señorita moving from one room to another in her big little house, replacing the flowers when they wilted, and thought of going over there to introduce myself. But I was just a paying guest. Besides, I didn't want to squander the dramatic possibilities of being grief stricken and alone in a foreign country.

"So loneliness is what you've got right now. Is that so bad? Why not want what you've got when you've got it?"

"But then I wouldn't get to sit around wanting something else."

"Like what, for instance?"

"Like a friend."

"What am I, chopped liver?"

"You're dead."

"I'd rather think of it as being temporarily without a body."

"Nothing against you, but I want a friend with a body."

"A woman, you mean."

"It doesn't have to be a woman."

"Oh no? Who do you think you're kidding?"

I took long solitary walks downtown, through the chicken district on Hidalgo, the yellow corpses strung feet skyward in the windows. Then came the plumbing supplies, tubos y conexiones, followed by the offices of dentists and purveyors of herbal remedies. Away from the zócalo and the tourists, I walked streets that did not show on the map, trying to lose my way and see things that otherwise I would not have seen: a woman snapping the dust from a rug in a doorway. In a barrio of narrow dirt streets on the far side of Calzada Niños Héroes de Chapultepec, named after the Mexican boys killed by American soldiers in "the halls of Montezuma," a white dog barked on a rooftop. Death was everywhere, of course, but there it was in the flesh, standing with his front paws on a brick parapet—singular, particular, incarnate.

Death was closer than any of us could know. You could step off the curb and be hit by a bus, as I'd once seen a woman killed in San Francisco. Just then braking to a stop, the bus seemed to touch her with no greater force than you would use to crack an egg against a bowl. Or, like Robert, you could go into the hospital at the age of thirty-six to get your plumbing fixed and never come out again.

Rosita prescribed sunlight and air for my athlete's foot. I sat in a beach chair in the courtyard under the white blast of the Oaxacan sun with triple-A flashlight batteries between my toes to allow the sunlight and air easier access. Singly and in couples, my neighbors at the Rancho, mostly retired Americans, came by to introduce themselves.

The French woman, Monique, arrived in a taxi late one afternoon and found me dozing in the beach chair.

"I am unique," I thought she said, but she had merely said her name. Dark skin, white hat and suit, nice body, held in a way that emphasized its niceness. Sweating from the taxi ride, her neck like freshly peeled mango. I recognized her at once as a woman in some kind of trouble.

"Do you need help with your bags?" I offered.

She raised her sunglasses and said, "You have something between your toes."

Ahead of me and Ramón, the caretaker, she led the way to her apartment, instructing Ramón to fill the water bottle, purify it with twelve drops of iodine—no more, no less—and check the cabinets for spiders.

"My life is in a chaos," she said. "The *jodidos* wouldn't let me take anything that I couldn't carry away in a suitcase. All lost. At this very moment they are touching my things with their filthy hands."

"Me too."

"Pardon?"

"My life is in chaos, too."

Monique stood back while I hung a mirror in the bedroom, its frame stamped with *milagros*—images of farm animals, for prosperity, and body parts, for health. When the mirror had been straightened satisfactorily, she said to it, "You may find it hard to believe, but I was once a beautiful woman."

The fireworks started about ten days before Christmas. They started deep in the valley and gradually worked their way up into the heights until it sounded as if bombs were going off in the street right outside the walls of the Rancho. The next revolution was starting, and the first to die would be the privileged foreigners cowering behind the walls of their *palacio*. But no—it was only the fiesta of Nuestra Señora de Soledad, Our Lady of Solitude.

A few days before Christmas, Naomi invited me to the Rancho's annual dinner party to celebrate La Noche de los Rábinos, the Night of the Radishes. After cocktails on the patio, we walked in a group to the restaurant. A pair of greyhounds were lying in the shade behind a cast-iron fence. One of them had cactus spines in its ear. Monique coaxed the dog to her, called her *pobrecita*. A servant came out of the kitchen, spoke to her through the fence, and returned with a pair of pliers. We watched solemnly until the last spine came free.

Monique and I walked back to the Rancho together after dinner. Her heels were giving her trouble on the cobblestones. Opposite the church she leaned against me, took off one shoe, and shook a pebble out of it.

"Are you married?" she asked.

"My wife's in the U.S. We don't live together any more, but we still see each other once in a while."

"The General wants me to go back to him. Never again."

We entered the Rancho through a carved stone archway consumed by vines. She took my arm and led me quickly across the courtyard, past the empty swimming pool that had sprung a leak thirty-five years earlier, according to Naomi. It had not been filled since then. Reptiles regularly got trapped in the pool and had to be removed by the help, and long ago, in livelier times, a drunken guest at one of the Señorita's parties fell in and broke a leg.

Monique opened a bottle of wine in her apartment, the only one rescued from her house in Jalisco—twenty bedrooms, cascading swimming pools, a landing strip cut out of tropical jungle, more than a mile of Pacific shoreline—a house in which, until recently, she had always been addressed as Doña Mónica.

The intruders came in the middle of the night, found Monique and the General in their bedroom, and told them they would be shot if they didn't leave the house within ten minutes. Some of them were local boys. They wore masks but were recognizable from their voices. The General had fought in Vietnam. These hired guns were pathetic, he said; it was obvious that they didn't know how to use their weapons. At first he suspected a certain politician in Colima, a man to whom he had offered food and hospitality in the past, who wanted the place to carry on a business in Bolivian heroin. Then he suspected everyone.

"When he went to the police, he was told that the title to the property had been transferred to 'an anonymous person.' It was against the law for *norteamericanos* to own property in Jalisco, they said; if he knew what was good for him, he would leave Mexico immediately. He went crazy after that. *Bastante loco.* He accused everyone of being part of the conspiracy. Even me. Eight years we have been married, and suddenly he thinks I want to steal from him. He said that it was over between us, so I came here. I have no other place to go—I have only my mother in France. And now, after all this, he calls and says that he wants me to come back. How can I go back to him now?"

After dark we took a taxi to the *zócalo*. Her perfume was the orange groves of Florida in full, unrelenting bloom. We sat knee to knee while she explained to the cabbie exactly where she wanted to be dropped off. I tried to remember when I had last been on a date—that particular anguish of the inner organs, the nakedness of one's imperfections. She took my hand as we drove into the city and guided it around her shoulder.

"Don't worry," she said. "I'm not trying to seduce you."

The *zócalo* was a solid wheel of people rotating very slowly around a hub of radish sculptures. A pompous radish politician was giving a speech to his gullible radish constituents. Just before the judges were scheduled to make their rounds, an entire family of artists were feverishly putting the last touches on a castle with scalloped red flags of radish skins flying from the turrets and an aluminum-foil moat full of radish alligators with gaping red gullets.

Monique pulled me through the crowd. "Incredible. After the fiesta, they will throw their castle into the arroyo with the garbage."

We found the others eating ice cream at an outdoor café near the *zócalo*.

"At last," said Naomi, "the happy couple. We were wondering what happened to you. Did you have time to see the sculptures?"

I'd come to Mexico in December to escape the madness of the holiday in the States and the disappointment that always comes with it. One could never be happy or generous enough. As it turned out, the *mexicanos* were even crazier than the *yanquis* when it came to Christmas. The fireworks scared away the melancholy that always shadowed the glad tidings—the knowledge that Christ, like the rest of us, had been born to suffer and die.

On Christmas Eve I was surprised to be missing my wife, Elena. I'd been gone for a little more than two weeks—not long enough to admit the triumph of longing for her over the longing to be alone, but long enough to consider how I was taking our separation. What I really wanted, more than to see her, was to long for her again the way I had longed for her before we were married, when she was in Poland and I was in the States, separated by circumstances rather than choice.

"*That's kind of complicated.*"

"I know. What are you going to do? Life's complicated."

"*Do you love her?*"

"I don't know. I loved her once upon a time. I still love the idea of her."

"*You should have married your idea.*"

Downtown I found a phone and called Elena, but nobody answered, so I walked over to the *zócalo* and milled around with the thousands, foreigners and *oaxaceños*, who had come to celebrate. The front gate of the Rancho was locked when I returned, but I'd brought my key with its wooden plaque, like keys to gas station restrooms in the States, too big to lose. It wouldn't fit in a pocket, so whenever I left the Rancho I carried it in a pack or ran the risk of getting locked out after hours. The word *GATE* was painted on the plaque with nail polish that had chipped partly away, leaving a ghost of the word. Instead of *GATE*, I read *GA-TE*, syllables from the Vedic text of the Heart Sutra, "the mantra which relieves all suffering": Ga-te, ga-te, paraga-te, parasamga-te. Gone, gone, gone beyond, completely gone beyond. We'd chanted it at Robert's cremation, and earlier, when he was dying in the intensive care unit at the hospital. How could a man who'd been so vividly in the world be so completely gone?

The fireworks didn't let up until well after midnight. Early Christmas morning, in the void between one day's commotion and the next, I dreamed that Robert was driving a team of Alaskan huskies across the vastness of the northern ice. He was wearing his black priest's robes, but he still had all of his hair. Icicles hung from his beard. The dogs were harnessed together with tattered accordions, and as they ran, they made a wild, spastic music—an Astor Piazolla tango. I called to him as he mushed by, but he couldn't hear or see me.

Monique showed up one night wrapped in a blanket with a plate of anise cookies and a bottle of French champagne. How often in this life does a once-beautiful, newly single woman in need of solace come uninvited to your apartment in the governor's mansion bearing anise cookies and wine? I'd been imagining just such a scenario minutes before she appeared.

She lit a stick of copal and solemnly offered it to the newlywed skeletons. "One day we must go to Mitla," she said. "It is a place of magic."

"Mitla? Isn't that where they used to cut people open with an obsidian knife and yank out their hearts?"

"Don't worry. I like you too much to kill you. Later, perhaps."

We sat in the living room on a painful wicker loveseat—except for the bed, the only place in the apartment where two could sit. She told me about the movie script she was writing that takes place during the Spanish conquest of Mexico. Hernán Cortés falls for the heroine, an Indian princess, but the princess loves another man, a beautiful Indian who never wore clothes in his life.

We drank and ate the anise cookies. Inspired by the champagne, I made a speech about root vegetables. Wasn't it funny that the Spanish word for potato, *la papa*, was like the word for the pope, *el papa*, especially since the pope looked so much like a potato himself?

She was resting her head on my shoulder. It would have been awkward not to put my arm around her. She placed her hand lightly over my heart, testing the strength of its attachments.

"Mi corazón," I said.

"No, no. *El* corazón. In Mexico your heart does not belong to you."

I considered wrapping her up in her blanket and sending her home, or inviting her to bed, and decided it was best to do neither.

"Tell me," she said. "How is it between you and your wife?"

"We were close for a while, before we got married, when she was in Europe and I was in the States."

"Do you miss her?"

"I missed her the other night. But it was like missing someone I'd known a long time ago, or someone who died."

"And men accuse women of being inconstant."

"You never know what's going to happen," I said helplessly. "Do you miss your husband?"

"I only wish that I could say no."

"Then what's the problem? He wants you back, doesn't he? So he went a little crazy. Everyone needs to go crazy once in a while."

"He was always crazy. But from that night on, when he saw that his power could be taken away from him by some little boys, he was a different person. I don't know him any more. I can live with a crazy man, but I can't live with a stranger."

"You call him 'the General.' Doesn't he have a name?"

"That's who he is. He lives life like a war that must be won, no matter what the cost. I have become a casualty in his war. He needs me, yes. He will always need me, or some other woman. But he absolutely loves his war. He loves his fucking landing strip. He will never stop being the General."

She put her head in my lap and wept.

"Robert," she said after the first wave had broken. "My darling Roberto. How can I live without you?"

Our Zen teacher, mine and Robert's, gave us this mantra: "I am surely going to die." Most people know it but don't believe it; that is, they don't know it *surely*. We'd rather not be reminded, much less reminded repeatedly, the way a mantra is meant to be repeated—not just as a way of remembering that death is inevitable, but as a way of inviting it to come and live with us, the way Mexicans invite their dead to the dinner table on the Day of the Dead. Living with the certainty of death is a sure reminder that life is for living.

When he finally decided to have surgery, after trying everything else the doctors had recommended, he probably didn't understand that he might die as a result, at least not with conscious understanding. Certainly not *now*, so soon. "Ulcerative colitis is a very unsexy disease," said the junior surgeon in the intensive care unit shortly after Robert died. "It kills a lot of people, but it doesn't get a lot of press." Or he knew he would die but refused to confess, to spare us, his friends and family, from useless worry. He hated being fussed over. What could anyone do that wasn't already being done? As he weakened, he kept up his Zen practice as much as possible, even though he'd left Baker-roshi by then and was struggling to understand his vocation as a freelance priest. He continued to drag himself to the café to see me, but instead of books, love, and Zen practice, we talked about his medications. His skin lost its color; he broke out in drenching sweats. One day he took so long in the men's room that I went to see what had happened and found him lying on the floor. "Just resting," he said.

Death was one thing we never talked about. We'd heard of it. We knew it was waiting. But the absolute certainty of the mantra evaded us.

Monique and I talked until late at night about our lost Roberts before she went back to her apartment. She came again the next day and recruited me for errands. Downtown, while she was getting money from the bank, I called Elena and left a message. We have to talk, I said. It came out sounding more urgent than intended, especially since I didn't know if there was really anything to talk about.

Monique found me in the *zócalo* and we sat on a bench while a boy shined her shoes. She hadn't brought any comfortable shoes with her from Jalisco, and she'd developed a blister on one heel.

"Everything changed after the earthquake," she said. "Before that we were happy. The General had his art business, and I was content to take care of him and the house. Besides, I had my script. We have earthquakes all the time in Jalisco—this is nothing unusual. The house wasn't damaged. But from then on it felt as if the world, my world, was starting to come apart."

I bought a bag of dried grasshoppers and offered them to her. Each red husk had been a living creature. A riddle came to me: What's the difference between a Buddhist priest who vowed not to harm sentient beings and an American general who swore to kill the enemy? Robert took his vows seriously. He wouldn't pick up a coin from the sidewalk because it would have violated the precept against taking what wasn't given. Once, half jokingly, I asked him if sperm cells were sentient beings, and he replied with a short "no." Robert seldom failed to elaborate. Only later did I recognize his teaching: Don't bother me with your discriminatory beliefs. It was as if I'd asked him to calculate how many angels could dance on the head of a pin.

"The General wanted to kill that notary in Colima. 'This man was not involved,' I told him. 'He's only taking orders from his boss.' But he went insane. I had to drag him away, or I'm sure he would have killed the man. After that, it was like he had gone somewhere else. We were still living together at the hotel, but I no longer recognized him. He refused to talk to me or even look at me. Suddenly I had become invisible."

The shoeshine boy removed one of Monique's shoes and handed it to her.

"Es mas chica," he said, smiling. One shoe was smaller than the other.

Elena was "seeing someone," she said on the phone—a "Spanish man." The first time they went out she'd told him that she wasn't interested in anything more than friendship. Of course, *he was*, whoever he was. I didn't need to ask or be told that because I was a man myself and knew how men were.

Why was she telling me this? Years earlier, when I was in the States missing her, she went to Norway to find work until I figured out what I wanted to do about us. "These Norwegian men all want something from me," she'd said. So I sent her a telegraph asking her to marry me. From then until she moved to the States with her children, she and I were as successful in avoiding the subject of our future as Robert and I had been in avoiding the subject of death. It was easier not to think about it.

"And what about you?" she said. "Did you make any new friends?"

"No. I thought I saw Robert on the *zócalo* last night. I ran after him but he disappeared in the crowd. Probably just a short German tourist with a shaved head."

"He's still with you, you know. He's watching you."

The phone booth was open to the street, and what with all the street noise—the fleets of drunken foreigners who sailed past, the traffic that stood and honked with the peculiarly good humor of nighttime traffic in Mexico, the music that leapt from boomboxes and doorways and car windows, the fireworks that hadn't missed a lick since Christmas—it was difficult to hear myself, more difficult yet to hear the woman on the other end. A young couple within a few feet of me, rapt in their attention to each other, were oblivious to all of it. He took a long drag on his cigarette and let the smoke drift slowly from his mouth into hers. She gladly took it in. I thought of how much this telephone conversation was likely to cost me. I thought of what Robert would have done had he been in my situation, and I knew it didn't matter because he was dead and I wasn't.

"Why don't you come down to Oaxaca for a while?" I shouted into the telephone. "We'll go to the beach."

One of the things that appealed to me about Monique—besides her fainting-couch theatricality, her shameless lack of interest in any drama outside of her own—was her absolute need to be with other people. In this she was unlike me and most of the people I knew, who habitually withdrew into private places, psychological and otherwise, if not into a pure solitude. She sought out company as naturally as I avoided it; it was exciting to be around someone like that, especially since I could pass my hand deliberately through the flame of her need without any danger of getting burned. Nothing ordinary was admitted into her life, which allowed me to think that I, too, might be more interesting than I knew, or failing in that, at least I might land an important role in her existential cinema. Everything that touched Monique had to be more elaborately staged and deeply felt than it could ever be in real life.

"Do you like her?"

"Yes, but it's hard to explain why. She's not the kind of person I'd expect to like. Quite the opposite."

"Why explain it?"

"She's so self-centered that it's almost funny. And she travels in society, the rich and famous. That's something I could never do."

"She's got a nice body for a woman her age."

"Yeah, I noticed."

"I wonder what she's like in bed."

"I've thought about that too. But that's as far as it goes."

"Why?"

"For one thing, she's married to a crazy Vietnam veteran who would probably kill both of us if he found out."

"And?"

"I'm married too. Did you forget?"

"Did you?"

"I promised to be faithful when I got married. Something along those lines, anyway. I'm not sure what I promised, to tell you the truth."

"Sexual faithfulness is part of it. If you think you're breaking your vows, then you probably are."

"What would you do, if you were me?"

"I'd do what I wanted to do."

"Thanks, you're a big help."

"That's not always so easy. And there's a catch. You're not allowed to hurt anybody."

"That's impossible."

"*Sure it is, but at least you have to try. You promised.*"

A traveler travels to experience the feeling of not knowing why he went, but knowing that he went for *something* and always being on the verge of meeting it. He doesn't meet the something if he goes looking for it, specifically, and he doesn't meet it if he stays home. But the very act of going prepares him to meet it, if and when it chooses on its own terms to make itself apparent.

I had the feeling that morning when Monique and I boarded the bus for Mitla. A thin man in a muddy tunic, grinning like he'd just won the trifecta, gave Monique his seat next to the driver. I had to stand. Each time the bus went over a bump my head slammed against the roof. On the outskirts of town an old woman muttered to the other passengers that she couldn't stand it any longer and insisted that I take her seat.

The Spanish missionaries had built their church on top of the temple at Mitla, tearing it down and building again with the old stones. They never finished the demolition, and parts of the complex remained unmolested, although mostly roofless, which after all was what made a ruin a ruin.

Monique forged ahead to the counter, where she convinced the ticket seller by virtue of her connections with certain officials in Mexico City, long since deposed or dead, that we were entitled to a discount. We walked along the length of an ancient wall, that is, the knee-high remnant that had not yet melted into the ground. Just on the other side, a dozen baby-blue party dresses hung from a clothesline.

Monique walked ahead with a provocative swing, but also with a hitch that I hadn't noticed until then, not quite a limp. Out there, in the unsparing light of noon, she looked more fragile than she did on the streets of Oaxaca and the shady pathways of Rancho San Felipe.

"Did you hurt yourself?"

"I have been hurt more than once. Years ago I was doing research for my script in the library at López Portilla's house. In the event of rebellion, the president had built a secret tunnel leading from the library to safety, outside the walls of the presidential palace. A trap door to the tunnel was hidden under a rug in the library, but someone had failed to close it. I stepped on the rug and fell through. I believe that López Portilla's wife, that jealous bitch, was responsible. She thought I was having an affair with her husband. Why would a woman like me want to have an affair with that old man? The president heard my moans and came with his personal body guard to remove me from the tunnel. I was three months in the hospital. Such pain I have never known. But I will tell you something. The pain of the body is nothing compared to the pain of the heart."

Clouds were piling up in the south, the first real clouds I'd seen in Mexico. The clouds might have been there for days or weeks, but cloistered at the Rancho, I hadn't bothered to look that far outside. A lizard held absolutely still on top of the wall, close enough to touch, as if stillness alone made him invulnerable. Robert had been a lover of reptiles and amphibians since he was a boy—"herps," he called them—captured them in the dwindling swamps and woodlots of suburban New Jersey and brought them home in his pockets. I envied this lizard his life among the ruins, the uncomplicated life of the body. Certainly there was fear behind that eye as it studied the tourists, but all I could see was stark, unemotional attention.

"Come," said Monique with characteristic drama. She took my hand and led me through La Sala de las Columnas, a rank of basalt columns bravely holding up the sky. The basalt was full of holes and looked as if it could have floated. One column had fallen. Myths of creation and destruction were written in the stone mosaics on the patio at the other end, the many things that priests knew about and were given to interpret—earth, sky, a snake with wings. A lone gust of wind carried a blessed mist into our faces, hardly more than a smell of moisture, then it was gone. Monique came close and gripped my arm tightly.

"The Spaniards called this place Mitla," she said. "It's from an Indian name which means Place of Death. People were sacrificed here. And they buried their leaders in tombs. We are probably standing on top of them right now. But for me, it's more a place of rest than a place of death."

"If you ask me, death is highly overrated."

"It feels especially peaceful to be here with you." She pulled away the skein of hair that had blown across her eyes and looked at me. "You know, I almost never feel peaceful when I'm with a man. This is something new."

Outside the plaza of La Columna de la Vida, a woman was selling *muñecas*, among them, a doll representing Subcomandante Marcos, the revolutionary leader of the Zapatista rebellion in Chiapas, two cartridge belts slung across his chest, his face hidden under a little black hood. Monique gave the woman a coin and we entered the plaza. Dust blew in thin sheets across the plaza and painted our feet its color.

"Here in the Place of Death the ancient priests made the Column of Life. You and I, together, must embrace it. If you feel the column move, it means that you will die soon."

"How soon?"

"Who can say? But if it remains motionless, you will continue to live—for a time."

"But will I live happily?"

"That's up to you. The gods don't care one way or the other."

She took two sticks of copal from her bag. We got down on our knees and made a house out of our two bodies to shield the lighter from the wind until the incense caught fire.

"Now," she said. "Stand here."

I stood facing the column on one side, and she stood on the other. Our hands met, encircling it, my cheek against the hot basalt. The earth did not move. Why I had been keeping this life at arm's length for so long was impossible to know, but perhaps it wasn't necessary to keep that distance forever.

After the ruins we had lunch in the little town. She called the waiter *joven*, young man. In Monique's world, it was necessary to keep one's place with servants. On the ride back to Oaxaca she pointed out the oldest tree in the world, closed to the public on Sunday. We traveled past irrigated fields, small farms of great beauty, a herd of sheep grazing under cottonwoods.

"Once I had a German lover," she said. "We had a jojoba farm in Bolivia. One day we were coming in for a landing in his DC-3. An old woman had brought a herd of sheep onto the runway, and it was too late to pull out of the landing. The plane plowed into the sheep. Many of them were killed. We went to the woman to apologize, but she wasn't even angry. We paid her more than the sheep were worth. The people came and took the bodies of the sheep and roasted them in pits in the ground. The whole village had a feast that lasted a week. Everyone was happy except my lover, who could think only of his damaged airplane."

"What ever happened to him?"

She threw up her hands, chaff to the wind. "He realized he was still in love with his wife and went back to Germany."

Elena's plane was an hour late arriving—right on time, by Oaxacan standards. It was like watching an old movie—the passengers in Central American period dress, panamas and double-breasted linens, a few military types in their civvies with leather briefcases, Indian women in tribal *huipiles*. They descended the staircase that had just then been standing alone on the runway, a staircase to nowhere, until two men in oily jumpsuits wheeled it to the side of the four-prop aircraft. Weary, hastily combed, sweating the instant they step into the sunlight, the disembarking passengers took their first draughts of that flowery thickness, the air of Oaxaca. Singly or in pairs they walked across the pitted tarmac to the terminal, where I was waiting with the others, friends and family, wives and husbands.

There was Elena in a skimpy yellow dress, carrying a daypack. When she'd arrived in Los Angeles with her two children, just before we married, I'd seen her like this, from a distance, before she saw me: the three of them and the heap of their possessions, literally everything they owned in the world, looking even more lost and frightened than I must have looked when at last they caught sight of me—the American man who was going to take care of everything. Although we didn't know it at the time, we'd already accomplished what we'd set out to do, and most of what remained was its undoing.

I felt a stab of desire when I saw her on the runway in Oaxaca. Or was it just a memory of desire, a last refusal to speak the truth of our situation? In her daypack would be copies of *Vogue* and *Cosmopolitan* purchased at the airport in New Mexico, a bottle of mineral water, a half-eaten box of marzipan, free samples of cosmetics collected from department store counters, one book or another about healing.

"Hello, Tom," she said, and gave me a friendly hug.

"Hello, Elena. You look good in yellow."

It was dark by the time we ate and took a cab to the Rancho. I'd forgotten my gate key—an ignominious start to the reunion—and stood on the street for ten minutes, pounding the gate with my fist.

"Are you sure this is the right place?"

"I've been living here for six weeks. Of course I'm sure."

Nobody came. I had to carry Elena's luggage all the way up to the church and around to the far side of the Rancho. That gate was locked, too. I pounded some more. We were about to give up and get a hotel room when voices approached from the other side. Ramón opened the gate. Behind him stood a tall, sturdy woman in a shawl with a wealth of silvery hair coiled on her head.

"I am Señorita Esmeralda Gastón y Sánchez," she said, smiling, as if being summoned to the entrance of her hacienda after dark by loud knocking were nothing out of the ordinary. "May I help you?"

I'm not much for the beach. Sun, sand, salt, the aimless hordes. It leads only to exhaustion. I went because Elena wanted to go and she was my nominal wife.

The ride south to the coast wasn't too awful for a second-class bus ride in Mexico, except it lasted four hours longer than the schedule said it would. We made a hairy descent out of the mountains, past agave farms and huts made of sticks and sheet plastic, barely holding on to the side of the hill, where the workers lived. After a few hairpin turns Elena felt sick.

"Mi esposa tiene náuseas," I told the driver, who nodded. Two miles farther on he stopped where some children were herding their goats, climbed over a stone wall, and picked a lime from the tree. He cut the lime in half with his pocketknife, instructed Elena to hold one half under her nose, and ate the other half himself. "Do not be afraid," he said. "Soon we will arrive in the sea."

We stayed at a pricey hotel in Puerto Escondido and sipped ruby-red margaritas in the restaurant before dinner—jungle decor and real parrots. They piped in the songs of Agustín Lara while we ate our over-priced snapper.

"Did you hear that?" I said over the Pineapple Mirage.

"What?"

"Agustín Lara just said '*mi corazón*.' There! He said it again."

"They always say this. They never get tired of saying it."

"My friend in Oaxaca told me that in Spanish it's incorrect to say *mi corazón*."

"You told me that you had no friends in Oaxaca."

"There, he said it again. My heart, your eyes—*como dos puñales*—like two daggers."

"I don't know this word."

"Daggers. Knives. Your eyes are like that sometimes."

"Yes, I know. They were not always like that, but ever since coming to your country, I feel that my eyes can kill."

That night we made love with a certain kind of urgency. It wasn't the kind we'd had long ago in that cheap hotel in Warsaw, my first night in Poland after a separation of months. This was the kind of urgency one feels while standing on the brink of a chasm, exhilarated, but wanting to retreat to safer ground as soon as possible. There was an annoying conviction of wrongdoing, too, as if my wife were off in another country and I'd brought a stranger to my room, someone I'd just met among the potted palms in the restaurant.

She wanted to stay there until we went back to Oaxaca, but I said it was too expensive, and besides, at the surfers' hotel she'd get to look at all the gorgeous boys on the beach.

"Yes, of course. This is the way you are. It's been so long we are not living together that I almost forgot."

By the time we got back to Rancho San Felipe, she'd had enough of me and Mexico, both. Mexican food didn't agree with her; neither did the ants in the bathroom. We were still together in our deluded way and would continue to be together for a while, until we stopped altogether.

The night before Elena returned to the States, we were getting ready to go out for dinner when Monique came to the door.

"Monique is one of my neighbors here at the Rancho. This is my wife, Elena."

She took Elena's hands in hers and squeezed them together. "She's very pretty, your wife . . . Señor, I have a favor to ask of you."

"Yes?"

"Do you have anything to drink?"

"I have a couple of beers. We were about to leave."

"May I have them? This man has come all the way from San Francisco, and I have nothing to give him."

"Your husband?"

"No, thank God. The General is in a rest home taking lithium for his *locura*. The art dealer is here. He's come to make me an offer for the Rodins."

"Auguste Rodin?"

"Who else? The General promised to pay me a commission on the sale. The collection once belonged to Pizinski."

"Another general," said Elena. "In Poland everyone loves this Pizinski."

"Then it belonged to Hermann Göring. Can you imagine? After the war, nobody wanted to touch it. They didn't want to have Göring's blood on their hands. The General bought it from the dealer, and now the dealer wants to buy it back for much less than it's worth. Other people are interested. The General has asked me to fly to Paris tomorrow and talk to them."

"The collection must be very valuable," I said, "especially with a history of ownership like that."

"About thirty million American dollars, maybe more."

"And if you sell it, what's your share?"

Monique looked at me and Elena confidentially, the way she might have looked at a couple of old and trusted servants at the General's mansion. "Between twenty and forty percent, depending on the price. I'll never have to worry again."

She took my last two beers and left to collect her fortune.

"This woman looks at you the way a wolf looks at a rabbit," said Elena. "Is she one of the friends you didn't make in Oaxaca?"

When you've lost someone, they say, it's a good idea to take a long trip to unfamiliar places, where loss will not assault you as relentlessly as it will at home. I'd planned to go to Mexico before Robert died, and I was lucky to be able to leave when all the memorial ceremonies were over—the seven-days ceremony, the cremation, the forty-nine-days ceremony, the poetry reading, the burial of his ashes at the monastery in Colorado—but before the unexciting fact of his death hit home.

Mexico's abundant reminders of death gave it a body and dressed it up in bright colors. They gave it a place of its own at Mitla; you had to pay to go in and see it. What was objectified or placed in the phenomenal world, the Mexicans seemed to be saying, held far less power over the living than the absence it represented. If you can see it, it's less likely to sneak up and grab you from behind. If it looks human, as in Spanish folktales, you can bargain with it, or outsmart it, or mock it.

Robert was everywhere in Mexico, as Elena had said he would be, keeping tabs on me. He felt more at ease in a country where distinctions between the dead and the living were not as strictly observed as they were at home, where those who loved him continued to stand in his way, wanting him to remain as he had been instead of being what he was now. He could drop by for a beer without feeling that he had to stay for dinner. All the things that would have delighted him in that country delighted me more because of him.

The hardest thing was returning to New Mexico and finding him still gone. He didn't show himself on the streets nearly as often as he had in Oaxaca, and over time he no longer frequented my dreams. I wore Robert's old sitting robe at the temple, the one he'd worn those years in

San Francisco and then in New Mexico before he got his head shaved and put on priest's robes. It was way too short for me; the fabric had been worn thin; it kept coming apart and continually had to be sewn back together.

On the weekends I played house with Elena. She said I had been "building walls" around myself from the day she arrived, trying to salvage what little remained of my money and my solitude. The demands of being a husband and a stepfather overwhelmed me. I felt like Jesus trying to feed the multitudes with two fishes and five barley loaves, but without his faith or compassion. I often remembered what Robert had said one of those times at our café, not long after Elena and her children arrived in the States: "You know, I have to tell you. You're a very loving person, but you're lousy at showing it. You're probably too scared right now to give everything you're capable of giving. So why not try giving ten percent?"

Two years after Robert died, I drove to Crestone Mountain Zen Center to visit his grave. We'd buried his ashes in a rock-lined crypt a short walk up the mountain from the monastery among piñons and junipers. The grave had been marked with an oblong rock, flat on one side and set upright in the ground, like the mountain itself. The gravesite looked so much like its surroundings that for a minute I entertained the idea that I'd dreamed all of this up—Robert, Robert's friendship, Robert's death. But there was his rock.

"How are you getting along?"

"Can't complain. Eternity can be kind of dull sometimes, but I'm in it for the long term. What's new with you?"

"Not a whole lot. Working. Still seeing Elena now and then. I miss you. I don't have anybody to gossip with."

"I miss you too."

"So why did you leave?"

"Because that's what people do. They leave. That's the one thing you can absolutely depend on them for."

"It doesn't seem fair. You love someone, and the next thing you know they're gone. Or if it's not them, it's you."

"*It's a bummer either way. But do you remember what you said to Monique at Mitla?*"

"You were there?"

"*Call it prurient interest. You were joking, of course, when you said that death is overrated, but you were right. It's really no big deal. Now, getting born again, that's a different matter.*"

Past Imperfect

IT'S BEEN TWO WEEKS SINCE THE AD FIRST RAN in the newspaper: "Extra nice studio apartment with sunroom and yard. $500 includes utilities."

"What's extra nice about it?" asks someone named Paula. I can tell she doesn't want it. She knew she didn't want it before she called.

"Well, you really should take a look. It's bright and cheerful. Good materials, good workmanship."

"And this is in a house."

"It was added to the house about six years ago as the master suite. My wife and I needed a place to hide from her teenagers."

"How many rooms?"

"Two rooms, one large, one small, and a full bath."

"But the large room is small," says Paula.

"About thirteen feet by eighteen feet."

"That's small. It's really an efficiency, isn't it?"

"I'm not sure what an efficiency is. But I guess you can call it that if you want."

"Sorry, I need more room."

I'm in the process of moving back into the house where my ex-wife and I lived before our marriage broke up. Today I'm putting out the garbage—mostly leaves from the backyard, freeze-dried dog turds left by the previous renters' dogs, and a few rattling locust pods—when Kurt Weiss, the next-door neighbor, ventures out, bent over from scoliosis, hands joined behind his back. His face and head are extremely red, as if freshly burned. It's been five years since I lived here, so it's not likely he remembers me.

"Hi, Kurt."

"Moving in, are you?"

"Yup, moving in again."

"The other people moved away."

I don't know if he means my ex-wife and her kids, who stayed in the house for a couple of years after I moved out, or the various groups of people who rented the place in the interim: the New Age deadbeats, into crystals and NFL football, who still owe me three months' rent; the string of employees of Wild Oats Natural Grocery, only a few blocks away, along with their friends and lovers and their dogs that clawed the doors and ate the windowsill. But what Mr. Weiss says is true, regardless of who he means. Everybody moved away.

"I live here alone," he says. "My mother died, poor thing."

"Yes, I know. I'm sorry."

He retreats into his yard, steps over the fallen Lombardy poplar that lies across the path to his door, as if he's long since accepted the fact of its being there. The top half of the tree blew down in a wind storm two weeks ago. The rest of it stands dead on my side of the fence. It's my tree, so it's up to me to haul it away. I am seriously considering the idea of cutting it up and putting it into bags for the garbage men to haul away.

Before deciding to move back into the house, I was thinking about selling it and buying another, maybe in town, maybe a little out in the country, and even got as far as telling a couple of real estate agents to be on the lookout for "depressed properties." Having gone in over my head to build the addition, I couldn't afford to live in the house alone. And I didn't relish the prospect of living in the kitchenless addition while renting out the rest of the house, heating up cans of tomato soup on a hot plate and shouldering my laundry across a vacant lot to the coin-op on Cerrillos Road.

One afternoon my friend Julie, who'd just moved to town and had never seen the place before, came over and walked through the empty rooms with me.

"This is very nice," she said. "How come you never said how nice it was?"

The last tenants had taken everything except a bag of pancake mix, which they'd left in the linen closet, and the bamboo wind chimes hanging in the apple tree out back. Julie and I sat on the back step in the cold February sunshine while she smoked and I told the story of the chimes—a gift from Elena before we were married. She'd moved in here with me when we first met, but then her visa expired and she had to go back home to Poland. We didn't know if we would ever see each other again. So she gave me the chimes as a going-away present.

"Burn them," said Julie.

I got a ladder out of the shed and unwired the wind chimes from their tree branch. Some of the pieces of bamboo were missing, and the ones that remained had split open and were gray and freckled with bird droppings. I got some newspaper and gathered cottonwood twigs from the backyard for kindling. Julie lit the fire in the fireplace. We stood in the chairless living room and watched the wind chimes burn down to ash.

It was Julie who came up with the idea of adding a kitchenette to the addition and renting it out so that I could live in the more spacious part of the house, with a real kitchen, three bedrooms, and a washing machine, instead of the other way around.

"You never thought of this?" she said. "Maybe you'd better give some careful attention to *why* you never thought of this."

I called my friend David, an architect, and asked him to help me plan the kitchenette. He had watched me agonize over the decision to marry Elena and take responsibility for her and her two teenagers from a previous marriage—three whole new people. At one point, when I was arguing with the city over a utility easement that stood in the way of the addition, David said, "Tell Elena you can't marry her because the sewer line runs too close to the house." He drew half a dozen floor plans and two complete sets of final drawings (the first was second-guessed by the builder), then made us a wedding present of the money I had paid him to do it.

Now David looked at the recess between the chimney and the bedroom wall, made a quick sketch, and handed it to me: a one-bowl sink and a two-burner cooktop over a half-sized refrigerator.

"The counter will be a little high," he said. "Just don't rent to any short people."

Those who come and look at the apartment politely tell me what's wrong with it, as if I didn't know already: It's small. ("Depends on what you're used to," I tell them. "I've been living in a closet for the past five years.") It's noisy. ("After a few days, you stop hearing the traffic.") There's no counter space, no oven, no washing machine.

I want to tell them the whole, unsweetened story. Right over here, on Cerrillos Road, you've got your Discount Tire. (Someone set fire to the pile of used tires a few years ago; it was really spectacular.) And over on the other side, Amigo Tire. Between the two of them, the air wrenches go all day long, six days a week. Directly in back, behind the fence, is the parking lot of the American Spirit Tobacco Company with its newly installed icy blue security light that shines in your window at night, as cozy as the yard lights at the state penitentiary. (Before the light went in, the police, on the lookout for a prowler, caught me climbing over the wall in the dark, instead of taking the long way around, past Pawn City, Mr. Tax, Weight Watchers, and the Berean Baptist Church.) The cul-de-sac turns into a lake during summer cloudbursts and can take a couple of days to drain. (Every summer it's the same. I call Streets and Sewers. Three men come out, open the manhole in my yard, look down in there, talk it over, replace the cover, and go away.)

To the right person, I could unashamedly, even fondly, confide these details, the things that make the house and its surroundings familiar to me, and therefore better to live in than somewhere unfamiliar. But the necessity of finding a renter turns me into someone I hardly recognize: a salesman, and not a very good one. When the skeptical women call, I hear the note of apology in my voice, as surely as I hear the skepticism in theirs. The really pleasant ones, I know without asking, have a dog.

Jan seems promising. On the phone she talks about the things that might disqualify her, instead of the things that will disqualify the apartment. She smokes, for one thing. Her world-weary voice, resigned, ravaged by tobacco, allows my ordinary, unapologetic voice to return. The other voices were too young, too wanting in experience. They were still ex-pecting life to be extra nice.

Jan makes an appointment. She's only the fifth who has actually come to look.

"How do you feel about a cat?" she asks after giving the place the once-over.

"I feel okay about a cat. One cat, I could see. I'm not sure how my cat will feel about it, though. I suppose they'll work things out."

"Mine is an indoor cat. That won't be a problem."

She's not as old as she looks. She's been chafed by weather and dis-appointment, but softened, rather than embittered by it. In this rounding off of the personality's sharp corners, I like to think we are similar.

"It's a clean little apartment," says Jan.

"Very clean."

"I'm only just starting to look. This is the first place I've seen."

"I get the feeling that there's a lot to look at right now," I say, defenseless.

"It's very nice," she admits. "But I'm just getting started. You shouldn't wait for me."

"Don't worry about that. I'm not waiting."

I'm building a fence between what will become the renter's part of the yard, on Mr. Weiss's side, and my part of the yard, on Mr. Spring's side. Mr. Spring, a retired engineer, also lives alone; his wife died a few years ago. He has a dog named Mitch who fetches the paper every morning and barks at me feebly when I'm working in that corner of the yard. The three of us—Mr. Spring, Mr. Weiss, and I—make up a little barrio of single men at this end of the cul-de-sac, vaguely aware of one another's comings and goings, cordial in our relations, but not inclined to chat across the property lines.

The new fence, made of vertical wooden slats, will enhance the pretense of separateness between me and my renter. It will follow the line of a wall that I knocked down right after buying the house, under the apple tree where the bamboo wind chimes used to hang, and perpendicular to the back wall, where I and my immigrant family watched the tires burn at Discount Tire—the greasy flames, like a judgment, curling into the nighttime sky. A troubling thought occurs to me: over the years I have been repeating myself, knocking down walls and putting them up again in the same place.

The fence breaks the customary flow of wind, creating a backwash in the corner. Other people's trash blows in from Cerrillos Road and settles in its lee: those substanceless plastic shopping bags that always snag on the powerline and in the branches of the apple tree. And the first page of a child's dictionary. The word at the top of the page is *abandon*: "to go away from without intending to return; to forsake completely."

A woman named January calls me at work to ask about the apartment. She has returned to the city recently, after three years in Montana on family business. I give her directions and permission to go in the yard and peek in through the big windows of the sunroom.

Late afternoon, she calls again and says she wants to look inside. She's already done her snooping, so she must know how small it is, and she has already seen and heard the unceasing traffic on Cerrillos.

"I'll be right over," I say.

January and a friend have parked the friend's Lincoln on the street next to the clogged storm drain and the black stain on the pavement where one of my renters used to drain his oil. Mr. Weiss has already received them at the curb and told them that his mother died. The four of us stand there in the street being neighborly. The fallen half of the Lombardy poplar in Mr. Weiss's yard has not moved an inch since the last time we talked.

"The man who used to live here is moving in again," says Mr. Weiss, meaning me. (I have not quite fully returned, have yet to reestablish myself as a member in good standing of the cul-de-sac.) "The other people had dogs."

January loves the apartment. Her friend likes it, too.

"Look!" rejoices the friend, whose name is Ivy. "Bookshelves! You'll have a place to put your books, January!"

January wants to move in right away, like tomorrow. Only one thing. She has a cherry red 1972 Mercedes that she is reluctant to park on the street: "Any chance I can park her in the driveway? She'll be a whole lot happier there."

Julie, among others, has warned me about the dangers of moving back into a house where you lived with a former spouse—the feelings of loss and desolation that might be resurrected, regardless of whether the marriage was a happy or an unhappy one.

"All that history is still there," she says. "You've got to change everything. Make the place look completely different from the way it was when the two of you lived together."

"What about my dining room chairs? Am I allowed to have them?"

"Where are they?"

"Elena's place."

"When are you going to get them?"

"Soon. As soon she agrees to be there and open the door."

"No. Call her up and tell her when you're coming over. Do you want me to come with you? It might be a little easier with another person. Less chance of bloodshed."

"No thanks. The blood's already been shed."

Elena lives in a rented house in Fairway Village. Despite the name, it's not much closer to the golf course than it is to the sewage plant. She comes to the door in a bathrobe, her hair up in a towel. She's thinner, if that's possible. Wearier, too. Maybe just weary of me.

It's been more than a year since I was here, not since that Christmas night. We had been living apart for a while, but we were still a couple. "Married on the weekends," was how a friend characterized it. After dinner, Elena said she had something to tell me. The two of us sat un-speaking at the dinner table for what seemed a very long time. I didn't ask, "What is it?" I just sat there studying the wine-stained tablecloth, waiting for what I probably knew was coming, at least on a gut level, if not in any conscious way.

Finally, she said, "I fell in love with Lawrence."

My first impulse was to correct her English: it might be better to say, "I *have fallen* in love with Lawrence." We had been over the difference between the past perfect and the past imperfect tens of times, and still she didn't get it. Action in the past perfect was over and done with. But imperfect action had a continuing and vital connection to the present, which I knew was the case here: she had fallen in love with Lawrence and continued to be in love with him, at that very moment.

No matter how she said it, there was no chance of any misunder-standing on my part. "I fell in love with Lawrence" told me everything I needed to know or would need to know in the months to come.

Now she unties the cushions from the dining room chairs, and I carry them out to the truck two at a time.

"Thanks," I say on the way out.

"Sure."

I think, *After all that's happened, there must be something more to say.* It's raining hard. I'll have to wipe off the chairs when I get home.

There's a new restaurant called Mu Du Noodles a quarter mile down Cerrillos Road, where the Natural I used to be. They serve "Pacific Rim cuisine," which confirms my faith that if you wait long enough and hold your ground, everything you need will come to you—even the Pacific Ocean.

It's busy at the Mu Du. I sit at the table by the window to watch the traffic and wait a full forty minutes before the waitress comes to take my order. She has the wise countenance and warmth of a mother, a face that for all its troubles—or because of them—can look directly into mine.

"I'm sorry," she says. "You looked like you were waiting for someone."

My Thai Girlfriends

IN THE DREAM I'M SERVED BY A THAI WOMAN wearing a white plaster mask. She and I are the only people in a large hotel dining room: antique table settings, six or eight to a table, and white linen tablecloths. The masked woman folds herself around me from behind, but along with the pleasure of being held comes the fear of impropriety. Foreigners are expected to practice restraint while visiting this country.

Upon waking, I write, "At my age sex may be a thing of the past, but to live well, it's best not to rule it out entirely. The desire, not the act, is the important thing."

A year off from work requires complicated arrangements. Someone must be found to replace me at work, where for fifteen years I've been editing archaeological reports for New Mexico's Office of Cultural Affairs. I'm worried that my replacement will not do the job as well as me, or that he will do it better. My house must be leased so I'll have enough money while I'm in Thailand. My medical insurance will be discontinued, putting me at the mercy of Asian diseases. I'll cancel my telephone, and the telephone company will give my old number to a stranger.

There's some explaining to do. It makes people nervous that I'm pulling up roots, leaving everything behind for a year. It causes them to question their own comfortable routines. They demand reasons. I say that I've always wanted to travel, which isn't true. The thought of going

alone to an unknown country terrifies me. I say that I want to experience a foreign culture, knowing that it's no more possible to leave my
own culture behind than it is to leave my own consciousness. Among
co-workers, I don't say that my leaving has more to do with the dis-
avowal of what I'm doing here than with anything I might find to do
over there, which might remind them of their own dissatisfaction. Nor
do I say that the real object of this adventure is not having to do anything at all.

One of the archaeologists at the office recommends Chiang Mai, a
city in the cooler, northern part of Thailand, as the best place to start.
Chiang Mai has everything, he says—great food, friendly people, antiq-
uities—and for Westerners, at least, it's incredibly cheap since the Asian
economic collapse. He tells me how to use the red taxis, which only
seem to be taking you miles out of your way. And he warns about the
beauty of Thai women: "It's okay to sleep with them, but don't get serious. You'll end up having to support her whole family."

The Kingdom of Thailand issues me a visa that's valid from July 23,
2002, until July 22, 2002, that is, minus one day. I didn't want to go to
Thailand all that much anyway, and now Thailand has complied with
my basic reluctance to visit their country by granting me less than no
time in the Kingdom. The Thais are famous for politeness, and "Please
come for minus one day" is probably their polite way of saying, "Don't
bother to come at all." I call the Royal Thai Embassy in Washington
D.C. and talk to Mr. Pop. He apologizes and says there's been a mistake,
which means I have to go after all.

As a going-away present, the Office of Cultural Affairs gives me a
lifetime supply of condoms.

It might be Saturday. I'm alone in Chiang Mai, sitting on the wooden
balcony that overlooks the courtyard of the Mountain View Guesthouse. Guests on the second floor are asked to walk lightly on the teak
floors to keep from disturbing those in the rooms below. There's no
view of the mountains, but Miss Daeng, the manager, says you can see
them if you climb to the roof of the building after a rain.

This morning two real estate agents showed me an apartment in a high-rise condo called the Embassy in the diplomatic district, across the river from the Old City. It was nice in a creepy way: the lobby encased in polished stone like a tomb, the Winnie the Pooh sheets on the bed, the baby-blue carpet, an extra bedroom for the people from home who said they would visit. From up there I could see the mountains, the green valley, the red rooftops of the city, clouds and sky, the brown river down below with shapes of things floating in it. Chiang Mai looks much better from the tenth floor of the Embassy than it does from street level, but I'd rather be down here among the leaves at the Mountain View.

A woman named Jessica lives in the room next to mine. She's from Tucson, Arizona, and has a horse named Happy, a buckskin mare, whom she misses. She loves animals and thinks that Thai people do not treat them with enough kindness. Other times she was in Thailand, she didn't see some of the things she's seen this time around. Maybe because the country was so beautiful and the people so friendly, she didn't see the unpleasant things on her earlier visits.

Jessica calls me Neighbor. I'm often sitting on the balcony over the courtyard when she comes and goes from her room. She's in Thailand to learn a therapeutic technique in which bundles of steaming herbs are applied to the body. She's buying the herbs in bulk and packing them in plastic bags to be sent back to Arizona. She's been talking to farmers in the region, trying to line up a reliable source of herbs for her business, but it's not easy to buy in sufficient quantities. Jessica has a large tattoo on her lower back, which I've come to think of as the *saddle* of her back, but I haven't been close enough to get a good look at it.

I ought to be seeing the sights of northern Thailand while I'm still a recent arrival here, otherwise I might become jaded and never see them at all: the orchid farm, the elephant camp, the snake farm, the water buffalo market, the umbrella village. One of the guidebooks says, "In order to experience the real Thailand one must leave the womb of the guesthouse," which I'm slowly preparing myself to do. For now I'm curled in the womb of the Mountain View Guesthouse with no view of the mountains, taking furtive looks at Jessica's tattoo and waiting to be born into the real Thailand. It must be here, within walking distance, and I'm convinced that it can be experienced by anyone with plenty of time to look, like me, or someone with less time but endearing personal qualities. I've been told that Americans are not yet hated here by the majority of the population—that if we are not exactly admired, at least we are looked upon with nothing more harmful than curiosity and envy. It's not the world outside that threatens as much as the task of being born into it.

Miss Daeng will know which of the sights in and around Chiang Mai are really worth seeing and which have been invented just for tourists. She and Jessica are in the lobby, a narrow space between the courtyard and the street decorated with sun-bleached posters of the orchid farm and all the rest. Miss Daeng is on the telephone long distance to India because Jessica needs to reach the teacher of some Indian martial art who might be willing to accept her as a student even though she is a Westerner and a woman. She wants to talk to him before traveling all that way for nothing, but Miss Daeng is having trouble getting through. Maybe the international telephone lines are tied up.

"Maybe India is closed today," I say.

She laughs at the joke. "Miss Daeng" (Miss Red) is her *cheulen*—a nickname. She knows a woman who has been called Miss Bank all her life because her mother worked as a bank teller before she was born and couldn't wait to get back to work after the baby was born. Miss Daeng is a short woman, even for a Thai, with disturbingly good posture. She's unmarried and has worked at her job as manager of the guesthouse seven days a week and all but two weeks out of the year for the past fifteen years, starting at six in the morning and finishing at nine or ten at night to support herself and her family, who live in Chiang Rai, another northern city.

"Maybe India is closed today," says Miss Daeng. "Ha, ha!"

Eventually she gives up and Jessica goes off to look for herbs.

"You're very kind to help your guests," I say. "You really ought to charge extra for your services."

"What do you mean?"

"In the United States people are paid for making arrangements for other people."

"How much are you going to pay me?" she says, sitting very straight in her chair. "One million?"

Jessica is buying a foot massage for Miss Daeng and Miss Nit, the guest-house cook, to thank them for their help, and I've been asked along. The four of us walk through the wet nighttime streets making jokes about our umbrellas. Miss Nit, a sinewy woman with dragon eyes, has the biggest umbrella. It's blue, and if it were the only umbrella among us, it would be big enough to keep everyone dry. Miss Daeng has the next biggest umbrella and the most beautiful, with its garland of red and yellow flowers. The two Americans have the smallest umbrellas, which is funny because Americans are bigger than Thais. My umbrella is crumpled from being turned inside out by the wind too many times. The women laugh at my sorry umbrella as we walk along the wet streets where families are eating.

"You've got to raise your umbrella awareness in Thailand," says Jessica, "to keep from sticking it in people's faces."

The sidewalks are choked with parked motorbikes and eating stalls, the paraphernalia of family industry spilling out into the public space from lightless interiors. A man sits in a black cell full of blackened gasoline engines that take up all the room there is except for one oily spot of light where he does the accounts. We walk past a floodlit, elephant-sized Buddha, past the Boys' School (girls are also allowed to attend), past ghostly temple courtyards closed for the night, and leave our shoes and umbrellas in the rain outside the massage parlor.

The masseurs in their green-checked uniforms are expecting us. The TV is on and stays on while we get our feet massaged. They smear our feet with Nivea and continually look over their shoulders to keep tabs on the action. Lots of shooting and fiery explosions. Jessica asks for the sound to be turned down. Miss Daeng translates from behind her newspaper. On the wall, a map of the human foot, its regions and municipalities, its major thoroughfares. When he's not watching TV, my masseur sometimes looks at me to see how I'm taking it. What I send back is my best imitation of a beatific smile even though his hands are very strong and just then when he dug his knuckles in I might have cried out in pain, but I didn't want to seem ungrateful or impolite.

The rain keeps coming down. My umbrella, left upside down, fills with water until it shifts and empties itself on the street. Next time I'll remember to leave it right side up, the way any intelligent person would.

Whenever I contemplate going somewhere else, getting on a bus or a train, I find reasons not to go. There's hardly enough time to travel out of town before my Thai language course begins. Anyway, what pleasure could there be in going alone, and in being so uncomfortably conspicuous in one's aloneness, which is hard enough to accept when it goes unobserved? A man alone in Thailand, native or foreigner, is an object of curiosity, if not suspicion. You do not eat alone in a restaurant, or you do it well after dark, when the restaurant is full of other people and your solitude is not quite so loud.

Night justifies sleep. In sleep I can forget who and where I am and all the things I am not doing here: crossing borders, exploring the track-less jungle or lolling on the beaches, chasing women, meditating, finding my way in Thai society, volunteering in refugee camps. I'm not doing much of anything besides walking aimlessly through the city. At night I sleep and sleep in the womb of the guesthouse.

The best time is between deep sleep and morning's first dove, when dreams can be read in the language of the waking mind. Cigarette smoke finds its way into the room, which means that the koi are being fed in their pond beneath the balcony. As always, the man who feeds the koi is standing at the edge of the pool with a cigarette and a cup of coffee, looking into the water. Jessica asked him not to overfeed the koi. She used to work in a pet store and knows that overfeeding kills them. The man listened to her advice and promised not to overfeed, but now Jessica has left for India to study martial arts and the man feeds the koi the way he always has, generously. When a koi dies, he ladles it from the water with a board that he keeps hidden among the plants next to the pond.

A few days before she left, Jessica decided to overhaul the koi pond. She and Nit and I took a taxi to the koi market and bought hyacinth and lotus and a few small koi to replace the ones that had died. I carried the koi in a plastic bag through the market where some boys were playing checkers with bottlecaps. Back at the guesthouse Jessica and I took off our shoes and waded into the pond and placed the pots of hyacinth and lotus where they looked best. Some of the pots would not stay put and we had to weigh them down with rocks and bricks. Then I opened the plastic bag and released the young koi into the water.

"How is your class?" asks Miss Daeng.

"Boring. All the students are men except for one Korean girl who wants to be a missionary."

We are expected to wear long pants and refrain from asking questions, which takes time that could otherwise be used for practice. I don't mind wearing long pants because it's cold in the classroom. Nobody is allowed to adjust the air conditioning except the teacher, Miss Patcharee. She warns against transgressions we, her students, have hardly had a chance to commit: coming late to class, not reciting when the whole class is asked to recite en masse, not studying at least one hour at home for every hour at school.

The bright young men show their exasperation with the dull-witted sybaritic retirees: "*Khun! Khun!* Don't you remember yesterday? *Khun cheu aray, kraap?*" Miss Patcharee smiles that deadly smile of hers, the one that says, "I'll make you suffer for your ignorance and sloth." Some of us recognize instantly that *rongraam* means hotel. Others must employ tricky memory devices. (A man enters the wrong room in a hotel and surprises a couple in the act of love. "Sorry, wrong room," he says. "Wrong room" sounds a little like *rongraam*.) We are taught the names of fruits that few of us have ever seen, much less tasted. Durian. Rambutan. Mangosteen. Miss Patcharee wants the Thai to leap immediately to our lips without any intervening mental process. English, we are told, doesn't have to enter into it at all. We will learn the language as a child learns it from his mother.

"Don't let me catch you saying *nung*," she says, and makes a foolish face. "When you say *nueng*, I want to see your teeth." She shows us hers, which were prominent to begin with. That deadly, patient smile.

The class gives me a reason for being in Thailand. Now when someone asks what I'm doing here, I say "studying Thai," a far more respectable answer than "sleeping and dreaming."

I experience a hunger for something sweet. Miss Daeng and Miss Nit are in the office at the end of their long work day, fighting off sleep. At this time of day their eyes are open but they can barely see.

Before going to bed Miss Nit lights incense at the spirit house, a gaudy miniature castle by the door where the guesthouse spirits live. When people occupy a place, the spirits who lived there first need a new place to live. Like people, they need to be cared for, fed, satisfied.

Miss Nit looks sexy even when performing a religious ceremony. George, an American with rheumatoid arthritis who's staying here, hired her to give him a massage even though she's the cook and doesn't know the first thing about massage. I would ask her for a massage, too, but it might be taken for an overture, and it might be one. What then? If desire is the important thing, then the act is not worth considering, and one had better stop considering it.

"Mr. Tom," says Miss Daeng, "what can I do for you?"

"I'd like two bananas, please."

"You have to ask me in Thai. If you want to learn Thai you have to practice."

"*Gluay song by.*"

Miss Daeng looks dully at me. She has fallen asleep sitting straight up in her chair. Either that, or I have forgotten to add the word at the end that makes it polite.

"*Gluay song by, kraap.*"

"Aaah," says Miss Daeng. "*Hok baht, kaa.*"

I give her the money. The bananas are small and starchy and sweet.

"Without question you cannot have conversation," says Miss Patcharee. She's right. I can't understand why this simple fact has escaped my attention for fifty-six years when I could have been having conversations with all sorts of people.

"You see pretty woman. You say, 'Hello, my name is John. I live in Chiang Mai. I come from America. I have motorbike. You are very beautiful.' No question. This is not conversation, *chay may*? So you must practice asking question every day in class. You must not be afraid to speak Thai. No one will laugh at you here."

I'm holding my own in the middle of the class, posing no challenge to David, the eager young American who teaches English to Thai children, or Sonjin, the Korean girl who intends to do missionary work, but managing to stay ahead of the dull-witted sybaritic retirees, such as Jeffrey, who's in his seventies and spends his evenings at the erotic massage parlor, and Howard, an Australian who's studying Thai so that he and his Burmese wife will have a common second language. The rest of us fall somewhere in the middle: Drew and Andrew, two young men who live in a Thai boxing camp where they work out seven hours a day, six days a week, and come to class beaten and exhausted; Peter, an expat Irishman who spends his time between Montpelier and Chiang Mai, depending on the season; Min, a Burmese political dissident who fled his country thirteen years ago during the crisis; and Nigel, a spherical Brit who stays up until four a.m. every night drinking beer and carries a business card that says "Professional Yachtsman."

By the end of class every afternoon I have a headache from concentrating too hard. But it's worth taking note of small victories: ordering *khao sawy* in a soup kitchen without menus, a place where foreigners don't go.

Improvements are being made at the Mountain View Guesthouse. The owner, who is also a doctor of herbal cures and a landscape architect, supervises the workers as they come and go. They're building a new entrance from the parking lot, a formal gateway made of the same red clay brick that was used to build the walls of the Old City. There are plans for a waterfall that will empty into the koi pond. The stream will course through a tangle of make-believe dead trees made out of plastered chicken wire. Experts in the on-site manufacture of dead trees are doing the work.

Meanwhile, business as usual. The old hippy, Pondo (short for Ponderosa), who proudly claims not to have worn shoes of any kind since 1970, shows up for breakfast first thing every morning. He has respiratory problems. With the end of the rainy season the air is getting worse, and he'll soon have to move to the coast, where sea breezes blow the smog away.

Young Christians have retreated here to study the Bible and do charitable work among the hill tribes. Every morning after breakfast the students, mostly German, meet in the building on the other side of the courtyard and sing loudly and joyfully for thirty minutes before studying the Bible until eleven. I envy them each other, their energy and youth. They sing as if they really mean it. One of the German girls has smoky eyes, and I try not to look at her too rudely from my place on the balcony.

The maids, whose nicknames mean Miss Beautiful and Miss Good, come every morning to make the bed and sweep up the droppings of the pale house lizards called *jing-jok*. Miss Beautiful once studied English and would go back to school if she didn't have to work. Yesterday she asked me if I was married. Today she asks me if I would be interested in meeting a certain friend of hers, an educated woman who has a good job selling textiles.

"No thank you, I'm not looking for a woman right now, I'm studying Thai."

"Oh? You study Thai language? *Waanii wan aray?*" (What day is it today?)

We haven't studied the days of the week yet, so she has to give me the answer. Today is *waan aathiit*, Sunday.

An old man with a mottled face and skull, wearing what my father used to call "carpet slippers," does his laps in the lane that runs along

one side of the courtyard, up and back five or six times, before allowing
himself to go home and watch television. He takes extremely small steps.
His feet slide along the wet pavement in the carpet slippers. He runs far
more slowly than most people walk, but he's running, nevertheless.

I meander across the campus of Chiang Mai University looking for the
bookstore. Since leaving the Mountain View Guesthouse and all the
way over here in the taxi I have been rehearsing, "*Kaw thot, kraap. Raan
nangseu yuu thii nay?*" (Literally, "I beg for punishment, sir. Where's the
bookstore?") Everyone seems to understand what I'm saying. The following conversation, more or less, is repeated a number of times as I
walk across the surprisingly large campus:

"I beg for punishment, sir. Where's the bookstore?"

"The bookstore?"

"Yes, the bookstore."

"The bookstore is over that way."

"Thank you, sir."

The bookstore is nowhere to be found. There is no bookstore, but
nobody wants to be responsible for disappointing me, this foreigner who
is trying so hard to speak Thai. What I find instead, by accident, is more
like a stationery store, where they sell T-shirts and coffee mugs with the
university insignia. I buy a pad of paper for homework assignments and
a note card with a picture of an elephant for Aunt Nancy, who lives in
Connecticut. She used to collect elephants of wood, stone, clay, and
glass but eventually got sick of having them all over the house and donated them to the Salvation Army. Back in the guesthouse, I apologize
to my aunt for sending her a card with a picture of an elephant. Thailand
is a land of elephants, I explain. It's almost impossible to avoid them.

A French woman, Nicole, is staying in the room that Jessica occupied
before she went to India. Nicole leaves her room early each weekday
with a cup of coffee in one hand, a satchel of massage equipment in the
other, her wine-colored hair tied in a no-nonsense ponytail. One afternoon she and I happen to eat lunch together at the guesthouse, and she

comments on the "pretty little bird" that is singing in the branches above the balcony.

"It's a red-whiskered bulbul," I tell her. "You can buy them in cages in the market."

"How terrible!" says Nicole. "The birds should not be in the cages."

"Well, you don't have to keep them. You can just give the people some money and they'll let the bird fly away. That way, everybody wins. The people earn some money, the bird is free, and you gain merit for your next lifetime."

"*Mais qu'il est barbare!* They should not be in the cages. They should be in the nature."

"Yes, I think so too. But this is Asia."

"I'm tired of it," says Nicole. "I'm tired of Chiang Mai. All the traffic! I cannot breathe here."

"Don't say anything bad about Chiang Mai to a Thai person. Chiang Mai is the Jewel of the North."

"Next week, after we finish the massage school, I want to travel."

"Where will you go?"

"I don't know," says Nicole. "To the mountains, where it's cool. Not too many tourists. I just want to be in the nature."

"Yes, I know what you mean. That's what I want, too, come to think of it."

"You should come with me."

Here's the company I've been wanting since I got here. She's sitting at my table and offering in no uncertain terms to go with me in search of the real Thailand. Someone to talk to, to negotiate with from one day to the next. Where to go? What to eat? To see the country through my eyes and insist on making me see it her way.

"I'd like that, Nicole. But I've got to finish school."

Miss Patcharee explains that Thai people are very curious and ask a lot of questions when they meet you. This is normal, she says: "In your country, it may be rude to ask somebody you don't know very well a lot of questions. 'How old are you? Are you married? How much money do you make?' But in Thailand, everybody asks these questions. This is how we learn who you are and how to speak to you. So when a Thai person asks many embarrassing questions, do not be angry."

We practice asking embarrassing questions in class. When Sonjin, the Korean girl, asks me how many Thai women I have, I say four.

"What are their names?"

"Daeng, Nit, Suay, and Dii."

Nobody knows that I've given the names of women who work at the guesthouse. It's easier for them to believe that I have four Thai girl-friends than that I have none. Thais and foreigners alike assume that if you are a single man from the West, you have a Thai girlfriend, or you are looking for one, or you are gay. Anything is acceptable except not having a Thai girlfriend and not even looking for one. If you say you have one or more Thai girlfriends, they leave you alone, but if you say you don't have a Thai girlfriend, they say, "You don't? Why not?" and then you have to explain. You begin asking yourself, "What's wrong with me? Why don't I have a Thai girlfriend like everyone else?"

Miss Patcharee teaches us the words for the different times of day. She explains that these words come from another time when there were no clocks, only the movement of the sun and stars across the sky. Nothing could happen at 2:45, for example, in the time before there was time; it could only happen in the afternoon.

"Now," she says, "you ask me question with morning, late morning, noon, afternoon, evening."

"Miss Patcharee," I ask when my turn comes, "what are you like in the morning?"

A new woman has joined the Bible students, and I've angled my chair on the balcony in such a way that I can keep a surreptitious eye on her. She's older, although not as old as me. Asian, although perhaps not entirely Asian. Her hair is short and very black; it shines marvelously. She's wearing a gray business suit with padded shoulders. She stirs a straw in a pineapple shake and listens intently to the German man, one of the leaders of the retreat, who is talking about a worldwide mission, going global in scale. Finally he stops talking and goes away. She's alone. She takes a book out of a black leather handbag and reads. I'm attracted to women who read because my notion of happiness includes lying in bed with someone reading. In this fantasy, we interrupt one another to speak only at long intervals, if at all. Our respect for one another extends to the other person's book. Right now while she's alone it would be possible to go downstairs and introduce myself. Everything would go well if I could remember to smile. If I smile too much she might notice that I'm missing a front tooth and draw conclusions about me from that, but if she is the kind of woman who draws such conclusions, I wouldn't want to be with her anyway. Anyway, she's too well dressed, too respectable, too Christian, and probably too married. The ring on her right hand. How would I appear to such a woman? A man with no apparent work or purpose in life other than studying a language that he will quickly forget when he leaves Thailand. A man who wears shorts and T-shirts and sandals, who rides songthaews or walks until the sweat breaks through his clothes. Just another of the aimless beer-sodden foreigners who spend all the hours after dark in tourist pubs looking hungrily at women. The only way I could distinguish myself in the eyes of such a woman would be to dress well and put on the guise of seriousness or ambition. The guidebook says that it's possible to reside in Buddhist temples in Thailand if one is a Buddhist or can "act like one." In the same way, couldn't one act like a Christian and win the admiration and maybe even the love of the woman with the shining black hair?

I pretend to be reading my book, which I got from the school library, to keep her from observing that she's being observed. Someone has left a scrap of paper in the book, probably for a bookmark, with a handwritten message on it: "Went to Soi 1 to investigate cushions."

Now and then, something turns loose in me, and I stop resisting the idea of being here. Then I'm yanked back into the resistance. The turning loose happens most reliably when I can make myself understood in Thai. I go to the airport to get my passport fixed. The woman in the immigration office smiles more than obligingly when I explain the situation in Thai, a smile of complete understanding.

"How well you speak Thai!" she says in English.

"*Khun paakwaan*," I reply. You're just sweet-talking me.

"No, no! Really!" She fixes the passport stamp and says that I can stay in Thailand until September, a full year from the date of entry. After that I can apply for another year, and so on indefinitely because I have a retirement visa. I can stay forever if I want. I could get a job at the university, have students who idolize me, buy a big shiny motorcycle and travel around, get a house in the mountains and hire handmaidens to cook and clean. Why not? Sit out on my own balcony in a rattan chair like a colonial lord and have the handmaidens bring me iced drinks.

After dark the desire for something sweet overcomes me again. Something sweeter than bananas. In order to get to the sweets from the guesthouse I have to cross Sriphum Road, wait for a break in the traffic, and make a dash for White Elephant Gate. There is no such thing as pedestrian right-of-way in Thailand. Just the other day an English woman was hit by a motorbike trying to cross here and sat dazed on the curb, refusing my offer of a chair, until the ambulance arrived.

On the other side of White Elephant Gate, a moat separates the Old City from the world outside, and then comes Mani Nopharat, another four lanes of constant one-way traffic. I push the button that operates the traffic light, the only one of its kind in Chiang Mai, and when the traffic slows I make another run. It must be done in a way to make the drivers believe that you really mean to cross and will not stop for anything, and then you have to watch for those who will run the light, regardless.

On the other side I move through a carnival of eating stalls, clear-glass light bulbs strung treacherously head high, starving dogs, giggling school-girls in uniform with large bows at the neck, men selling shots of whiskey from a bottle on a wooden crate, a woman in tribal dress carrying a wok filled with rocks on her head, whole families, whole villages, all eating and talking, and not one person among them who knows me.

All at once I realize I'm in Asia. It's been here all along, no farther from the guesthouse than a mad dash through the gate which isn't a gate at all but a gap in the ancient wall, wide enough to admit a herd of elephants, an absence, incapable of keeping anyone out or in, invading armies or lone tourist in the throes of a midnight sugar fit. All it took to get here was the risk of my life.

With a bag of sesame candy I move through the pandemonium, survive the return crossing, and reenter the guesthouse. Miss Daeng and Miss Nit have gone to bed. The night clerk is snoozing at his desk, and out on the wooden deck in the courtyard, where the half-formed shapes of ferro-cement trees lie fallen by the koi pond, the woman with the shining black hair is eating watermelon and reading a Bible smaller than the hand that holds it. She is so intent on her study that she does not look at me as I pass, nor does she offer me a slice of watermelon. On her perfect ankle, like volcanic islands in the process of being born, is a chain of mosquito bites.

I tell Miss Daeng that I'll be leaving the Mountain View when my Thai class ends.

"What's the matter?" she says. "Are you boring?"

"Yes, I think that's the problem."

The rain wakes up a gecko, or what I assume to be a gecko, having never heard one before, a clack like two pieces of wood being struck one against the other, or water dripping into water in a cave, greatly amplified, or an old dog that has lost part of its voice. People here kill geckos because they're noisy, I'm told, but nobody would dream of complaining about the two small dogs at the end of the lane who throw demented fits of barking at all hours of the day and night.

The rain excuses sleep, and sleep puts off my need to make better sense of all this. It's not really necessary to make sense of it, in the way that eating and sleeping are necessary, but I *think* it is, and the thinking creates its own kind of necessity. Making sense of things—for example, my compulsion to hear the word "gecko" in the mechanical grunts of a lizard—is human and forgivable. So I'll forgive myself for thinking, as I'll forgive myself for going back to bed on a rainy morning. I'll lie in bed listening to the "possible" gecko, as they say at the Office of Cultural Affairs. It may or may not be what I say it is. I'll listen to the rain on the guesthouse roof as sense departs.

After a night of heavy rain, the canal has flooded, and water is standing in four rooms on the ground floor. A nation of cockroaches emerges from flooded drains. Stunned by the light of day, displaced and having no other place to go, they collect on the walls, the branches of the manufactured trees, the tables and benches in the courtyard. They observe the guests and delicately taste the air with their long coppery antennae.

The staircase to the roof is opposite Miss Daeng's desk. It has been here every time I passed through the lobby to Sriphum Road over the past two months to walk along the canal or catch a songthaew, but this is the first time I've troubled to climb it. Three doors lead from each landing, rooms usually occupied by missionary students, all of whom have successfully avoided me for two months, except in passing, and I them. They've all left for two weeks in the mountains to sleep on mats on the ground and eat the food that the villagers eat and talk about the Bible. Their final exam.

The staircase ends at a wooden deck where potted plants have been allowed to grow wild. Vines cling to the wire of a dovecote and meander between runs of pool-blue plumbing. The cook, Miss Nit, is there on break, smoking a cigarette. She leans against the parapet and watches the traffic on Mani Nopharat plow through the flooded street. Sometimes at night I've heard her screaming at her daughter, presumably for the same kind of reasons that parents scream at their teenagers in my country, and found it strangely comforting, a reminder of home in a land where it's considered rude if not disgraceful to show anger. Miss Nit's toughness shows in those dragon eyes at all times, even when she's enveloped in steam in the kitchen, and now, in the enticing way she leans over the parapet, pulls the smoke from her cigarette, and releases it into the air.

"So much water," she says in English. "Too much."

"Where I live, there's never enough."

"It's dry?"

"Very dry. It's so dry that the trees are dying."

"I cannot live in so dry country."

The mountains are slowly coming out of the clouds after the storm. Nests of fog have snagged in the trees of the lower slopes, and higher up, behind a veil of vapor, I can barely see the white ramparts of Wat Phra That Doi Suthep, the first place one is expected to visit as a tourist in Chiang Mai. I stand there on the roof with Miss Nit and watch the clouds dissolve.

"Have you ever been to the United States, Miss Nit?" ("Without question you cannot have conversation.")

"No. I want to go with my daughter. I would like to see your country. I would like to travel in different places and see different things. It must be wonderful to do that."

"Wonderful, yes."

"Where do you go now?"

"I don't know. I have to decide. Or maybe I won't decide. Maybe I'll just get on a bus and go."

"This is good way," says Miss Nit. "You visit Doi Suthep?"

The veil of cloud is lifting from the temple now. It stands newly washed and dazzling in the late afternoon sun.

"I've been too busy with my Thai class and everything. But I want to go soon, this week, before leaving Chiang Mai."

"When you go, please burn incense for me."

"Why don't you come with me? We can both burn incense."

"Thank you, but I have to work. You will burn incense for me on Doi Suthep?"

"Sure. Do I have to say anything?"

"No. Just light incense and think of me. Then give it to the Buddha."

Dawnyen. Evening. Soon the jing-jok will stake out their places on whitewashed walls all over the city and begin their remorseless hunt for insects.

134

The Man Who Gave His Wife Away

CHAW DUMPED A WHEELBARROW FULL OF CORNCOBS on the fire and made a lot of smoke. This was Asia, and in any season Asia did not come without smoke: smoking fields of rice stubble, smoking timber slash, smoking motorbikes, old men and women smoking cheroots.

His two brothers had left home when they were young to look for work in the city, but Chaw stayed in the village. He had seven children and another on the way, he said, rubbing his potbelly. It was hard to guess his age. His face was too smooth and free of worry for a man with seven children.

The couple from the Alps and finally the sisters from South Africa, quieted by the unexpected cold and overnight nicotine withdrawal, joined us around the smoky fire to smoke. Today we would climb higher in the mountains and visit Chaw's friend—"if he's home"—a scheduled stop on the two-day trek.

"Who was snoring last night?" said Frédéric, a florist from Toulouse.

"It couldn't have been me," I said. "I was awake all night with the roosters. It must have been Andre."

An electrical lineman from the Italian alps, Andre knew no English, but he knew he had been accused of something and put on an exaggerated mask of innocence.

"Maybe it was a panther," said Chaw. "They can make a sound like a man snoring."

"Right," I said. "One of those blonde South African panthers."
The two sisters, Simone and Shantelle, clutched their cell phones and
smoked. Shantelle was under suspicion: she had the more pronounced
nose of the two and wore braces on her teeth. It was a little disappointing to have come all the way from America, to have sought out a
corner of Thailand where few tourists went, to walk for a day through
tropical forest and sleep in a thatched hut, and in the deadest, blackest
hour to hear only the manic roosters and the dainty snores of a girl from
Johannesburg. No jungle noises. Not so much as a bird or an insect. I'd
seen and heard more wild nature on the streets of Chiang Mai.

"Sometimes a panther will come into the village to steal chickens,"
said Chaw. "A boy was attacked not far from here, in another village."

"Really?" said Simone, the blonder sister. "Was he hurt?"

"Only a little. The panther bit his neck and let him go. Maybe it
thought he was a big chicken."

The trail followed a steep, sparsely forested ridge. From up there
we could see the congregation of thatched roofs that was the village, the
smoke from half a dozen morning fires rising blue in the still air, a boy
launching himself on a bicycle from a plywood ramp, oblivious to the
foreigners watching from the hillside.

Chaw stopped often to rest: "I must go slowly because of the baby."
He carried a machete on his belt and a basket with our food and water
on his back. Where the ridge leveled out he stopped again to cut two
lengths of bamboo for walking sticks. He carved one end of each stick
into a whistle, kept one for himself, and gave the other to me. Because I
was the slowest? The oldest? Did I look like a man who needed a walking stick?

I'd seen this kind of thing before in Thailand. On another walking tour, the guide had stopped repeatedly to make toys from plants: a
winged crane from a blade of grass, a hairy flower head transformed into
a spider that did pushups, a branch from a banana tree fashioned into a
hobby horse, a tiny seed pod that snapped open in your hand when it
touched water. Plants were interesting in the eyes of tourists because of

the amusements that could be made from them; animals, like those little crabs that lived under rocks in the stream, because they could be eaten.

Chaw blew into one end of his stick and made a soft green sound.

"Now you," he said. After a few tries my whistle made the sound too. We continued along the trail, Chaw in front, me at the rear, talking back and forth on our whistles. Of course, this was why I had come to Asia—to walk along a trail in the forest playing a bamboo flute.

Where the slope eased and the shade thickened, Chaw stopped and blew three long notes. He waited a minute and blew three more. From a place far down the dark side of the mountain a voice answered. Then I saw the faint track, a slight parting of the leaves, a barely perceptible flattening of the ground that led us down into deeper forest along a tributary ridge, the line of slowest descent. Every now and then Chaw shouted down the mountain, and each time the answering voice was closer. I couldn't tell if actual words were being exchanged or only shouts, but their meaning was clear: "I am here. Where are you?"

We came out of the trees onto a knob, just a momentary leveling of the slope. Sitting on a floor of banana leaves under a leanto of sticks and banana leaves were five dirty people: a man, a woman, two boys, and a girl. The three children looked about the same age, none of them older than eight. They sat before a dying fire with a thick rind of white ash around it. It had been cold enough in the village where we had slept on a raised floor of wooden planks with mattresses and blankets; it had been colder here. The five people sitting in their house of banana leaves, really just a surface to reflect the heat from the fire, had no bedding and little in the way of clothing. The man wore only a rag, the woman a cotton skirt and T-shirt, the children T-shirts and nothing more. None of them wore anything on their feet.

The man grinned when Chaw spoke to him—a bony little guy with folds of loose skin hanging over his ribs. He sat at ease, his feet out in front of him. A fringe of hair circled his otherwise naked skull. His face looked shrunken and collapsed, like the face of a man who had forgotten to put in his dentures, but when he grinned you could see his white and perfectly even teeth, the teeth of a film star. One ear lobe opened in a wide loop: an earring made from an ear; the other had no hole in it but had been stretched in such a way that it hung in a doughy ball and swung free.

The woman was not comfortable. She wasn't used to visitors and did not look at us. She sat crumpled next to the man, her legs folded back and under to one side so that the weight of her body seemed about to topple her. We stood there gawking, wanting to hide ourselves from her embarrassment—or was it closer to outrage?—not yet able to see, much less comprehend, who and what we were seeing. There was no way to leave until it was time to leave, no way to turn away and stop looking, to relieve her of the painful weight of our attention. She picked something out of the girl's hair. The children looked at us with more fear than wonder. We were new but not in any way entertaining. Like their mother, they had not learned to disguise their wish for us to go away.

Chaw took a package wrapped in a banana leaf from his basket and handed it to the woman. She said something but did not look at him, either—this man from another tribe who had been born in these mountains and lived his whole life here and even spoke a little of her language. He was yet another foreigner, although not quite so foreign as the rest of us with our expensive cameras and hiking shoes and packs sewn in Thailand and sold overseas before returning with us to their native country. She opened the banana leaf and took out the gleaming strips of pork fat—a gift, or payment in exchange for services? The woman loaded the fat into a length of green bamboo, plugged the open end with the banana leaf, and placed it to steam on the fire.

"They only want the fat," said Chaw. "They won't eat pig meat."

Shantelle offered the woman a bag of snack food she'd brought from the city, the Thai interpretation of something made in America. The woman took it without a word or a hint of recognition—no curiosity, no sign that something had been given and received. She did not once examine the present but held it in her hand and looked to the right and the left and behind her, as if searching for a place to put it away, some way to deal with its strangeness, and finding none, let it drop unprotected on the ground.

Chaw lectured. There were not many Mlabri people left, perhaps fifteen or twenty families. They lived in the mountains and hunted, sometimes in Thailand, sometimes in Laos. They went back and forth between the two countries without passports. They didn't have villages. They didn't raise animals or grow food. They didn't wash. They didn't get sick, or if they did, they knew which plants would cure them. They didn't trade with strangers or touch money. They moved from place to place according to the season and what they could find to eat. The forests that were their home were being cut down. The government of Thailand had tried giving them houses to live in and rice to eat. They didn't want houses or rice.

Chaw spoke to the man in the man's language, which he had learned from him the way he was learning it now, one word at a time: knife, food, rain, child. He spoke to each of the children and made them say their names.

"They don't keep the same children all of the time," he said. "The children go back and forth from one family to another." They married with the same kind of liberality, until the woman decided to go with another man, or the man with another woman. This was ordinary behavior for them. They never got jealous. They knew sadness, he said, but not jealousy. Once a Mlabri man's wife died. In sympathy the man's brother gave him his own wife. The brother missed his wife so much that he cried for three days.

The pork fat was ready to eat—still white and raw, but hot. We stood there in the clearing that was no more than a slight opening in the trees, hardly enough room to park a pickup truck, and watched them. When he was done eating the man took out his pipe and loaded it with some dry leaves from a pouch. His fire kit consisted of a flint; a rectangular piece of steel that had been cut from a machete blade; and a wad of cottony tinder, the fluff from a seed pod, kept dry in a bamboo tube. He held the flint in his fingers, the tinder nesting just below it in the bowl of his left hand, and struck the flint with a sharp swipe of the steel edge. Fire leapt into his hand. The tinder began to smoke.

Certainly it would have been easier to light his pipe with a burning stick from the fire, but then we would not have seen him perform his magic, and he would not have had the pleasure of showing it to us. Chaw managed to strike a spark, but it wasn't enough to catch the tinder on fire. If I had tried, I would have missed and cut my hand to the bone with the wild man's steel.

Besides the clothes they were wearing, the fire kit which they carried in a bamboo flask, and the pipe that the man was smoking, they had two machetes, both lying on the ground on the floor of banana leaves. There was nothing else—not a single cooking pot. The few objects before us were all that they possessed, with the exception of a spear with a hafted steel blade which the man no longer showed to anyone from outside. He had shown the spear to a Thai person once before, and allowed him to touch it. After that the hunting was bad. Now he kept it hidden, to save it from corruption. When the family moved from one place to another, they took everything they had with them.

"Maybe this is why they have so little," said Chaw, "so they won't have to carry it." Then it was time for us to continue on our trek and the Mlabri family to resume their ordinary, unseen life. I wanted to know what they planned to do for the rest of the day, now that their appointment with Chaw and his clients was over. If they were walking to another place, would they carry on a conversation as they walked, or sing, or make jokes, or be very quiet and listen for the voices of birds and animals? Did they follow known paths through the forest, or was it better for any reason, or none, to go a new way? Were they afraid of snakes? Did they know ahead of time where they would sleep that night, or did they just stop when they were tired? Did they have names for each other that were different from the names they told other people? What was the very last thing the woman would say to her husband before they slept that night? But none of it was my business.

Frédéric asked permission to take pictures, and the rest of us fell in alongside him with our cameras. I had a throw-away Fuji I'd bought in Chiang Mai, a small concession to the law that one must take pictures when visiting a foreign country. The man and woman and their children sat impassively as we snapped away, as if they didn't know they were having their picture taken, or didn't know they were participating in whatever we were doing, or knew and didn't care.

We left the family sitting where we had found them and climbed back up to the ridge, to the place where Chaw had warned them of our approach with his bamboo whistle, and walked further along the trail. Each of us wanted to make some private sense of what we had just witnessed, to find something to compare it to in previous experience. No matter if they had already gone on their way, paying the careful attention to where they stepped that people without shoes do, or were still sitting in their house of banana leaves, talking about where they would go and sit next. They were always at home, couldn't help being home, except when people came to look and put them in a strange place.

Shantelle saw a vine that looked like a snake. "It *is* a snake," said Chaw. Bright green, it hung head down from a green vine so that the two of them, vine and snake, looked like one and the same being. Chaw probed it with his walking stick until it dropped to the ground and disappeared.

We came out of the trees into a sunny clearing, a lychee orchard, where I took a picture of the expedition. The trail went down steeply from there, and then we were walking on a dirt road. We entered the village where our driver was supposed to meet us. Soon I would be returning to the States—my house, my job, my cat—ordinary life.

In the village we waited for our ride in the shade of a small pavilion with a corrugated steel roof, which served as a place for town meetings. A few teenagers stood around drinking Cokes. There were a couple of benches, and some of us sat a low adobe wall out of the worst of the heat. The chill of that morning was the memory of another place and time.

"Thank you," I said to Chaw, handing the walking stick back to him. "Maybe someone on your next trek will need it."

Flying home over the Pacific, I found myself missing that musical walking stick—my wife and companion for two days in the hills of Southeast Asia—and wished that I hadn't given it away so casually.

Integrity

WHEN AUNT NANCY DIED, we planned to meet at her house and caravan to the graveyard in Woodbridge, Connecticut, for the burial service. The last of her generation, having outlived her husband by eleven years and her sister (my mother) by twenty-five, she deserved a procession.

In a curious lapse over the telephone, I mistook "Nancy's house" for the house in Woodbridge where she had lived for most of her married life and where as a child I had come to know her and Uncle Roy on family trips to the Connecticut countryside. Each time we crossed the bridge over the Housatonic River on the way to Roy and Nancy's, tires moaning on the steel grill of the bridge span, we sang out, "The gre-e-e-a-a-at Housatonic!" We never failed to notice, some distance downstream, the figure who perpetually swam in it—the River Boy. Didn't he ever get tired?

The house stood in the middle of a rolling field that had been cleared and planted by some Yankee farmer generations before my aunt and uncle moved there to work for Olin Mathieson in New Haven. Walls of black fieldstone had been rough-laid on three sides of the clearing, probably by the same farmer. One of those walls marked the boundary between the cultivated land, endlessly mowed by Uncle Roy on a riding tractor, and the swamp behind the wall, descending to the Wepawaug River.

Of course, "Nancy's house" did not mean the house in Woodbridge, which had been sold to strangers twenty years earlier, but the apartment in a housing development known as Heritage Village, in Southbury, where my aunt and uncle moved after they retired. I knew better, having been to Heritage Village infrequently over the years to sit with Nancy in her living room and catch up on news of the family (she always knew more than I did about what everyone was doing). But in one unrevised district of my brain, she was still tromping around in her swamp boots behind the stone wall, admiring her young Christmas trees and pointing out a curl of fox scat to those of us who'd tagged along. So when my brother-in-law said we would meet at "Nancy's house" and process to the graveyard in Woodbridge, my first thought was of the two-story frame with the blue-gray clapboard siding in the middle of a mown field, the fieldstone wall that ran along one side of the driveway leading to the garage, the smell of cut grass and gasoline when you got out of the car, and the funny handshake Uncle Roy always gave me, working my arm up and down like a hand pump.

Nancy's house? But someone else lived there now. What were they going to think when a bunch of long-faced strangers pulled into the driveway?

Recently there had been signs that my aunt was no longer reliably herself, at least not the one we had come to know and marvel at over six decades, who led those expeditions into the wilderness of the Wepawaug; who raised bees and harvested honey in the comb (it won't hurt you to eat the wax, it aids in digestion); who planted a baby giant sequoia among the Christmas trees—an unthinkable, almost unchristian act in that neck of the woods, since everyone knew that giant sequoias belonged in godless California; who dug clay with her two hands right out of the earth and threw pots in the basement; who fired at woodchucks from an upstairs bedroom when they had the audacity to approach her garden; who had always been the soul of industry, good sense, and good nature, treating us children those many days we romped in her earthy paradise, me and my two sisters, almost as if we were her own.

Was she no longer quite herself, or was she herself more than ever, only magnified to unmanageable and therefore scary proportions? When

I'd called in February to tell her I was coming to visit "whether you like it or not," she couldn't hear me over the telephone—so I hoped—or she didn't know who I was. ("It's Tom! Your nephew Tom!") In either case I had to call three times before she seemed to understand that, whoever it was, was coming to see her regardless of her wishes and yes I knew that she was unable to feed me and anyone else I might bring along, a warning she had been giving for years to anyone foolish enough to venture into her precincts around lunchtime. To be sure she understood, I mailed her a postcard naming the date and the visitors—me and my daughter, Hannah.

This was the first indication that Nancy might be less than sound in body and mind. (I will call her Nancy—Roy's pet name for her—having known her as Nancy all my life, even though she rebelled against the indignity of it in her nineties and wanted to be known by her given name, Anna Catherine.) Besides being ninety-six, there was nothing wrong with her that anyone could tell, although a case of shingles had set her back a few years earlier, and we knew that at that age she couldn't stay perfect forever.

Nancy wasn't one to divulge her age, and *wouldn't* the time I asked point blank how old she was, since she had fallen under suspicion of shaving a couple of years off the true number. Either she didn't want us to notice that she was getting old and to think or act accordingly, or else she was punishing me for never having remembered her birthday in the almost sixty years she had been my aunt.

She had been testy with me ever since I wrote about a hypothetical fruitcake that a hypothetical person's hypothetical aunt might send them for Christmas, which, as good and sweet as it might be, was way too much to eat. She *had* sent me a fruitcake the previous Christmas, but not the one I'd written about. No criticism of her fruitcake had been intended—I'd happily eaten half of it before taking the other half to the office.

"You can't fool me," she said. "That was not a hypothetical fruitcake. That was *my* fruitcake. I'd know it anywhere."

Even in her nineties, she resisted the notion that her age was of any interest, since there were so many more interesting things to know about her. If one simply failed to notice how old one was getting, others might fail to notice, too, and old age might be circumvented altogether.

"How are you?" I always asked when I called, something I might have hesitated to ask an aged person other than her, since the answer might remind them of things they would rather not think about.

"Well, I still have my integrity," she would say. "What about you?"

For reasons unknown or undivulged, Nancy and Roy didn't have children of their own. Ignorance leads to speculation. We blamed Roy, who reliably mixed the martinis and mowed the lawn, but suffered the reputation of a hard-working but dry and unimaginative man among his in-laws. Anyone would have suffered by comparison to my aunt. They may not have been able to have children for one reason or another. Or they may not have wanted children. Children can be a lot of trouble—a fact that Nancy became painfully aware of sixty years ago and was reminded of a few weeks before she entered the hospital and, finally, the nursing home where she died.

When my mother went to Sloane Hospital in New York to have me, my sisters Penny and Valerie, then seven and five, were delivered for safekeeping to Roy and Nancy's place in Norwalk, Connecticut. The girls had a great time, said Nancy; she didn't. One afternoon she drove them to Calf Pasture Beach in the Model T to go swimming. They sat in the rumble seat, and every time the car hit a bump they shrieked with delight. Aunt Nancy, who had little if any previous experience of children in the absence of their parents, was daunted by the weight of responsibility that had fallen on her. Somehow she lived through it, but the trauma of having to deal with my shrieking sisters on the road to Calf Pasture Beach may have been the thing that decided her once and for all against children.

She enjoyed her privacy. I can't remember staying overnight when we visited Nancy and Roy in Woodbridge, and none of us ever stayed in the extra bedroom while visiting her in Heritage Village. Nor were we asked. Family was to be cherished and, as much as possible, avoided. Please come whenever you can, and please leave before dark.

My aunt and I shared a finite tolerance for family. It wasn't that she and I disliked hanging out with our relations, within limits, but we liked being on our own as much as or more than we liked our occasional to-getherness. After Roy died, she declined offers from both of my sisters to live with them. Knowing her own nature as well as she did, she recognized and forgave similar tendencies in me.

"You and I are a lot alike," she said. "We're autonomous."

Nancy may not have liked that I lived so far away and could only manage to visit now and then, but she understood it, as she understood and accepted the compromises that our autonomy sometimes entailed, such as loneliness.

Once she called me with a proposal—the first of only two phone calls I ever received from her. Roy had been dead for some time, and after a second divorce I was living in a very small room in a Buddhist temple, opening the door at 5 a.m. every morning and sweeping up rice in the meditation hall after the rowdy Tibetans.

"We're both alone," she said. "I have an extra bedroom. Why don't you move in here with me?" And then, to emphasize that her motives were more practical than personal, "We could share the expenses."

I said I'd think about it, but I was too much like her to seriously consider such an arrangement. Before I had to say no, she called again to apologize and say how embarrassed she was.

"I don't know what I was thinking. You'd be miserable here. It would never work."

The next time I visited, I brought her a present of a Japanese temple bell, the kind used in meditation practice to signal the beginning and end of sitting periods. She learned how to strike it, and how to make it sing by circling the wooden striker on the bell's rim, like a finger on a glass harmonica.

Then she asked me to show her how to meditate. I put a sofa cushion on the floor and assumed the half-lotus posture.

"What do you think about when you meditate?" she wanted to know.

"Nothing in particular. Whatever comes into your head. But you don't dwell on your thoughts. You just let them come and go."

"Is that all there is to it? I've been doing that for years, in bed."

Although I've always loved and admired my aunt, now that she's gone I discover how little I know of her life, including the eleven years after Roy died when she continued on her own in Heritage Village, apparently a paragon of self-sufficiency. When the two of them were still alive and well, it didn't occur to me to wonder how she occupied herself, since that other person was always there to know, and it was enough to know that someone knew. One of the dangers of married life is that it allows others to perceive the marriage as a small but sufficient universe that doesn't need to be known by parallel universes. We, the others, stop paying close attention.

A man or woman alone is more likely to excite curiosity. My aunt dispensed scraps of information about her life as a single woman without going into much detail. I know that she liked to watch television and was an avid, lifelong fan of the New York Yankees. She took their wins as manifest destiny—they only *deserved* to win—and their losses as a sign that the natural order was grievously out of balance. I'd grown up rooting for the Brooklyn Dodgers and couldn't find a shred of sympathy for the Yankees, even when they were losing, so out of mutual respect she and I avoided the subject of baseball. I know that she voted Republican, and rather than getting mad at each other, we avoided the subject of politics, too. I know that sometimes she woke during the night and lay in bed meditating, or composed poems and limericks in her head. Sometimes she wrote them down, but when she looked at them in daylight she usually decided they weren't any good and threw them away. I know that she did low-impact exercises every day, drank hot chocolate, ate defrosted low-calorie dinners. I know that she regretted not being able to make pottery any more, not being able to knit, not being able to drive—this woman who had driven the Model T and reluctantly gave up driving only on the advice of grownups, when she was ninety-three. I know that she maintained a keen interest in us, her nephews and nieces, including the long-lost nephew who, for reasons unknown, maybe because none of us came to his wedding when he remarried, turned his back on the family and never spoke to any of us again—not even Nancy, the oldest and most innocent among us, who'd never gone anywhere even when she was able. The mystery nephew had taken her habit of guarded independence to an unforgivable extreme.

She seemed happy enough, maybe even happier without having to worry about Roy, but for her, the authentic measure of well-being was closer to honesty than happiness. It was okay to be unhappy as long as you were honestly unhappy, instead of trying to put it aside. She often badgered me for facts when I called ("As usual, I'm doing most of the talking"), but what she most wanted to know was the condition of my mind and spirit. If she sensed that something was troubling me, she demanded to know what it was. With a parent I might have tried to avoid the issue, but she required the truth and would not be spared from it.

"You've told me almost everything," she said once. "Now tell me the rest."

After my mother died suddenly—and then, after a long incapacity, Roy—Nancy seemed satisfied to keep tabs on us and our families from a distance. With her in Connecticut and us in Detroit, Chicago, and New Mexico, we posed little threat to her autonomy. Widowed and living on her own, if she had been asked to make a choice between having her relatives too close and having them too far away, she probably would have chosen the latter. So it came as a welcome surprise when, in her nineties, she took to calling us hers.

"I think of you three as my children," she said unequivocally each time I called.

We had done nothing to deserve our promotion, unless it were to be unfairly left without parents—as she had been left without her brother, sister, and husband—when the parents of our contemporaries weren't even starting to get old yet. Certainly she saw in us the children she hadn't been able to have, or hadn't wanted, or had wanted in some part of her being but not badly enough to justify the trouble and expense. Over the considerable distance that separated us, perhaps we could be trusted to give her, besides the love of children for a parent, what she most wanted from her few remaining years—not to be interfered with.

It started with an altercation between her and Millie Truelove, a neighbor she had hired to buy and deliver her groceries. Millie bought the wrong kind of frozen dinners instead of Nancy's kind. Something like that, anyway. Nancy fired her, leaving herself in danger of starvation, or so we thought, since she was no longer able to leave the apartment. (We learned later that she had stashed away enough food in her closets, mostly instant oatmeal and hot chocolate, to survive at least the coming apocalypse, if not the next one after that.) My sister Valerie had to call Millie and patch things up on Nancy's behalf. Soon Millie and Nancy were friends again. But we, her designated children, agreed that her behavior, while typically stubborn, had not been typical enough, and we'd better keep a close eye on her.

When Hannah and I went to see Nancy, without a doubt she knew who we were, but otherwise she was in poor condition. She was thinner and weaker and slower than before. The skin on her legs was in terrible condition; they looked as if she'd recently been rescued from a fire. She, her clothes, and her apartment all needed cleaning. When I offered to find someone to come in and help, she said no thanks, she was taking care of things on her own. She seemed happy enough to see us, although less happy than in the past, and less sad than usual when, after a visit of barely an hour, I saw how tired she was getting and said we had to go.

Clearly she needed help, but what kind, and more to the point, how were we going to convince her that she needed it? On their next visit with Nancy, Penny and her husband decided it was time to intervene. Apparently Nancy had been having "ministrokes"; a neighbor, concerned when she didn't answer the telephone, had found her in bed and unwakeable. My sisters undertook the unpleasant mission of traveling to Southbury for "the takeover." There they told Nancy that they had arranged for someone from the agency to come to her apartment three times a week to help her out. The unmentionable alternative was for her to enter a nursing home.

"I don't need help," she said. "Millie brings me my groceries and everything else I need. If I need help, I've got my beeper."

The next day Penny and Valerie introduced her to her new helper and left the two of them alone in the apartment to get acquainted. Fine, no problem. She seemed to accept the idea of having a stranger in her house. In fact, she was pretending to be good long enough that everyone would go away and leave her alone. When the helper came a second day, she'd had it with the pretending. She threw the woman out. She accused my sisters of trying to kill their old aunt. Worse than that, they were violating her privacy. On the telephone with Millie Truelove, the two women she had recently taken to calling "her children" were now referred to as "those girls." With the catastrophe of Calf Pasture Beach still fresh in her mind sixty years later, she told Millie, "I wish those girls would go home."

They did go home, as they had planned, but they didn't give up. When the agency sent another helper, thinking that Nancy might get along better with someone different, she called the police and reported that there was "an intruder" in her house. The police came. The neighbors came. People were standing around outside the apartment trying to figure out what was going on. Heritage Village had never seen such excitement. On the telephone from Detroit, Penny was trying to explain to the police what an uninvited stranger was doing in her aunt's apartment.

Meanwhile, her integrity bruised but still intact, Nancy sat inside watching the Yankees game on TV. They had been in an awful slump lately and needed her full support.

The Woman in Question

HERE I AM ON THE WESTERN SHORE OF LAKE MICHIGAN thinking about a certain woman who is one thousand five hundred miles away, more or less. Nothing certifiably romantic has happened between us, but I can't stop thinking about her beautiful laughter.

I called to ask if she wanted to come out here to Sturgeon Bay, Wisconsin, and visit me for a while. She sounded interested but had a work deadline in a couple of months and other plans after that.

"Then I might have to find some excuse to visit you there," I said. "My cat probably misses me. He lives pretty close to you, come to think of it. The people renting my house are taking care of him while I'm away."

"What's his name? Sorry. I'm not trying to change the subject."

"That's okay. His name is Max. Some relation of Max Factor had him when he was a kitten."

"Max is a good name for a cat. Better than Factor, anyway."

"Maybe I left a burner on at my house."

"Soup's probably hot by now."

"Oh my God, the soup!"

By the end of the conversation, we still didn't have a date, although we clearly intended to have one at some point in the misty future. Two months? Three? Much too long, at least from my perspective, sitting here at the lake with the seagulls. However long it takes, I'll be waiting for

the time to pass so I can see her again, and waiting is something I promised myself never to do. Why wait for something illusory when you can
have exactly what you have right now—the deadpan lake, an inch of cold
tea in the cup, this heavy solitude—and not have to wait at all? Waiting
is nowhere, but Sturgeon Bay, Wisconsin, is somewhere real and specific, with many appealing aspects yet to be discovered. Last year at this
time, I was waiting for my year off to begin, so I could do more or less
what I'm doing right now, minus the waiting.

There wasn't much going on here in May, before the summer people start to arrive. A week passed before I saw anybody walking on
the beach—a woman bundled up in foul-weather gear who obviously
couldn't wait to get back inside. The red light went on in the driveway,
out back of the house, so I called Septic Man to pump out the holding tank, but he came and went without introducing himself. When I
went for a haircut at Joe's Barber Shop, Joe didn't even ask what kind
of haircut I wanted; he'd been giving the same one for thirty-four years
and knew how it was done. I thought of checking out the local pub, but
people don't go out much around here weeknights, and what would they
have to say to an outsider who doesn't even like to fish?

One sure way to avoid waiting would be to get in the truck and
drive back to see her, except then it would look like I didn't have anything else to do and was just driving back to see her, which is to say, it
would look too much like what it was. Better yet, I could fly out there
tomorrow or the next day and take her to dinner. On a plane I'd cross
in a matter of hours the distance it took four days to drive coming the
other way. I took back roads and stopped often to eavesdrop on the talk
in roadside cafes ("If he ever wants to get going on that job he'd better
get started"). In Oklahoma I found a recreational area next to a duck
pond and put up a tent. It was early in the season, and the only other
camper was an unemployed sheet metal worker from Minnesota who
was going fishing to wait out the economy. He'd been on a charter boat
that sank in a storm on Lake Michigan—a terrifying experience, he said.
Thankfully, nobody drowned. He asked to be remembered to the skip-

per, Vince somebody from Sturgeon Bay, if I ran into him while I was out here.

Dinner is a possibility. But what if it doesn't work out? What if she's bored to death by my rapturous descriptions of Wisconsin in the early spring, the music of love-drunk frogs pulsing in the swampy woods, those little flies that swarm over the clearings like smoke? What if she decides as a result of our long-distance date that I'm not potential boyfriend material, like that other woman, the anaesthesiologist from Florida, who flew out to see me for a long weekend and left the next day, having decided in the brief time between her arrival and departure that I would never become a surgeon, and who remarked bitterly on the way to the airport that my dog needed a bath? Then I will have wished that I stayed here thinking about the woman in question instead of traveling all that way just to be disappointed.

Taking everything into account—the distance between me and her, the newness of our friendship, her deadline, and the fact that my cat has not troubled himself over me for one second since I walked out on him nine months ago—I wrote her a letter saying I'd decided to tough it out here for "a while" and do what I'd set out to do before she entered the picture: write, read, ride my bikes. I didn't let on that I would be waiting all that while, however long it lasted, to see her again, or that I had not been able to stop thinking about her since we met. She wrote back saying she was happy for me but "sorry" for herself, a sentiment that causes me to reconsider: it wouldn't do for a woman like her to be sorry on my account.

Many people my age have outgrown this kind of thing, and for the past year and a half, for the first time in my life, I started to fear that it was happening to me, too—that I'd finally used up my lifetime allowance of love and it was time to enter an era of more sensible pursuits: writing, climbing mountains while I was still able to climb them, making more and better friends of either sex. What a relief to be liberated from the whole tragicomic struggle of wanting and not getting, or wanting, getting, and losing, which could all easily be avoided by not wanting in the first place! Love is too much damn trouble, far too demanding of time and energy. Just think what might be accomplished in the post-love era. I'd learn to dedicate myself to something totally new and uncharacteristic, like doing good works, with the same intensity that I'd dedicated to love in the past. I'd shine so brightly in my liberation that women wouldn't be able to resist me.

Then I sat next to the woman in question at dinner with friends in New York. We drank wine and ate sushi. She was so lovely, so warm, so rich in her attention to everyone and everything, that I knew there would be consequences for me of one kind or another, soaring bliss or abysmal misery, and probably both. On the way uptown in the cab to drop her off, I mentioned that I was "looking for something to do" in New York for the next few days before flying back to Wisconsin, and if she wasn't "all booked up" already, would she be interested in "doing something" with me? She was. Notebook and pen leapt from my shirt pocket, I wrote down her number, and at that instant, somewhere on the nighttime streets of the Upper West Side, all of my resolve to live a life of virtuous independence went straight to hell.

We went to the Metropolitan Museum to learn about the influence of the Spanish painters on the French painters. She studied the paintings, and from a respectful distance, I studied her—a paintable woman if there ever was one. She disappeared in the galleries, which made perfect sense: I'd dreamed her up, and now she had returned forever to the kingdom of dreams. No, there she was in front of *The Annunciation*, a dubious look on her face as she regarded the cherubs piled up like wood shavings around Mary, who was just then receiving the word from on high: "Guess what? You're pregnant."

We spent the day getting lost and unlost, which was a large part of the pleasure. Having asked a museum guard how to get to southern Asia ("turn right at the Medusa"), I placed a paternal hand on her shoulder, meaning to show the way. But nothing I said or did, no matter how confused or awkward, was reason for anything other than shared amusement. Walking back across Central Park in the warm afternoon, we saw an eight-foot-long yellow and white python, someone's pet, lounging on the new green grass. I couldn't decide if the grass was so green because the python was so yellow, or because this woman had mysteriously opened my eyes to the color of things.

Two days later we sat on the steps of the Public Library, intending to see the sonnet exhibit, and talked for an hour or more before going inside. Then she wanted to eat oysters in Grand Central Station, so we walked east. I was so engrossed in our conversation about the meaning of "Wurlitzer" that I almost walked right past it and might have kept walking all the way to the East River if she had not gently suggested that Grand Central Station might be that building right across the street. (I grew up in New York and drove a cab there. I know Grand Central Station when I see it.)

Later, heading downtown in the subway to visit Ground Zero, she asked for my address in Wisconsin.

"Are you going to write me a letter?" I said like an idiot.

"Then you don't want to give me your address," she stated.

"No—I mean yes!"

Her postcard, which arrived a few days after I returned to Wisconsin, was what gave me the courage to call and ask her for a date. Hanging out with me in New York had been "delightful," she wrote. But exactly how delightful had it been? The card didn't say. Was she as delighted as I was, or was she just being polite, like when you write your aunt to say how delighted you were to get the fruitcake she sent for Christmas, which you then take to the office for the buzzards to devour? And what about this "Love," capitalized, followed by a comma, written in front of her name. Was it the same old kind of love that people always signed in front of their names, or a hint of another kind yet to come?

She and I continued to write and talk on the phone at long intervals. Whole days went by without a word in either direction, and sometimes as many as three or four. She wanted to take "one thing at a time," she said when I tried making plans to meet her later this summer. What was the "one thing" she had in mind?

It wouldn't do to call on weekends. She might be seeing someone, and she'd know that I wasn't. Once or twice I thought of the dark-haired Bulgarian waitress in a neighboring town to whom I'd said, "You don't look like you're from around here" when she served up the breaded whitefish special, but more as a way of diverting my attention from the woman in question than from any significant interest in the Bulgarian waitress.

There were times when I could hardly remember what she looked like, but even then, I remembered too well how it had felt to be close to her. I remembered, too, who I had been when I was with her: a man I liked immediately and wanted to know better. Nothing seemed to take my mind from her for very long. Not the long bike rides on county roads through Wisconsin farmland, intended to make me so hungry and tired that the thought of anything besides food and sleep was more than I could handle. Not the pileated woodpecker that flew across the road during one of those rides, a giant compared to any woodpecker I'd ever seen, and a bird that not even the natives saw often. Its dazzling red crest brought an unconscious shout of amazement out of me. Then it was gone into the trees, and in no time at all I was thinking not of the miraculous woodpecker but, again, of the woman fifteen hundred miles away who was working on her contract and for sure having stimulating social encounters without me.

Maybe the trick was to give in to the waiting, rather than trying to gainsay it or call it something else: caution, maturity, strategy. Maybe the waiting itself was the important thing. For two weeks, I consoled myself with the thought that if, by some impossible chance, she walked through the door and threw herself into my arms, this delicious hunger, the feeling of sitting here longing for her, would be gone. Too bad that in the midst of longing, it always seems such a poor substitute for who or what is longed for. No question, it was far nicer to sit with her that afternoon in Grand Central Station, eat oysters, talk, and hear her beautiful laughter than it is to sit here thinking about it.

Then came a paltry excuse. Some people I didn't know—a Lutheran minister, his wife, and their dog—were coming to stay in this house on

Lake Michigan where I've been so conscientiously waiting and thinking. They were wonderful people, I was told; their dog was a wonderful dog. It was a big house, three bedrooms and two baths. We could all share it happily for the two weeks they planned to stay.

I called the woman in question and told her about these rowdy Lutherans who were about to ruin my peace and quiet. "Wisconsin is starting to get to me, anyway," I said. "I'm eating bratwurst and saying 'you betcha' to the checkout ladies at Econo-Foods. So if you're going to be around in three weeks or so, I'd like to take you to dinner."

She agreed. Neither of us acknowledged in words what we both knew, that I was planning to cut short my retreat by six weeks, load up all my gear, and drive one thousand five hundred miles just to take her to dinner, and for no other reason.

In my next letter, I added recklessly at the end, "When can I start saying inappropriate things to you, like how beautiful you are?"

She wrote back, "Plus or minus fourteen days."

I replied, "Sorry, can't wait that long. You are astonishingly beauti-ful." As soon as I mailed the letter, I knew that I'd spoken too soon and said too much, even though what I had said was obviously true, and besides that, true to what I felt. The word "astonishingly" repeatedly slipped my memory in the days that followed. It was too painful to be reminded of my clumsy come-on, which had been more like a slap in the face than a caress. How beautiful had I said she was? Astoundingly? Devastatingly? Outrageously? For days I dredged up the letter and sub-jected it to withering critical review. What an ass! Why did I have to go and say anything? There would have been plenty of time to tell her how beautiful she was at the right time, when I got there, when I was actually beholding her beauty.

A few days later she replied with a postcard, Bouguereau's painting of two young angels embracing. It was close to two in the afternoon. I stood in sunlight next to the mailbox on Lake Michigan Drive. Birds were probably singing in the woods; I can't really recall. On the back of the postcard was a message: "I loved your letter & I want to kiss you: I want to kiss you."

There are still a few days to go before I leave. Four, exactly. The things that I've been doing up to now to wait out the waiting—refinishing doors for my brother-in-law, driving into town at every opportunity to check e-mail at the library and pick up some bananas, watching the NBA playoffs, obsessively cleaning and lubricating my bikes—things done to take my mind from other things and cheat time into passing more quickly than it would have passed otherwise, are now performed like a dance, to music. The waiting has turned into something closer to patience.

Things will have to be eaten in the refrigerator: the purple asparagus bought from an angelic blonde farm girl at a roadside stand. She said some people thought the purple was a little sweeter than the green. I still haven't done anything about the copper teakettle that suffered a meltdown and lost its spout that night I got on the phone with the woman in question and forgot the water heating on the stove. The house is clean enough, but I'll clean it anyway and water the potted flowers that won't be watered again until the Lutherans arrive. Then, come Tuesday, I'll get up very early in the morning and drive like mad to her door.

The Pending Disaster

"I CAN HARDLY BELIEVE IT MYSELF."

Anne, my girlfriend, is talking to a neighbor on the phone while I open a bottle of wine in the next room.

"You can hardly believe what?" I ask when she's off the phone. "Sorry, I couldn't help overhearing."

Her hesitation. The look of being caught off guard. "Not that I'm getting cold feet or anything. But what if I move in with you and it turns out that we liked each other better before? It's not like we can go back to living separately again and everything will be the same—you said so yourself."

The theory goes something like this: lovers move forward together toward an unpredictable future, or they try to maintain the status quo, or they split up. Anything's possible except returning to a former state of innocence or happiness or shared ambition. People aren't made that way.

I hand her a glass of wine and propose a toast: "Here's to cold feet. May they take us wherever we really want to go."

My father, Bernard Patton Ireland, wanted to be a writer when he was a young man. He went to graduate school for a while before taking a job in the admissions office at Columbia, where he worked for the next twenty-five years. Job, marriage, and children pretty much put an end to his writing ambitions, although he continued to write speeches for his work and was known in college-admissions circles as a witty, entertaining speaker. I can see him at the dining room table drafting his next speech on a yellow legal pad.

One of the few pieces of his writing that survives is a journal he kept from when he was in graduate school until shortly after he married my mother. It begins in 1936, a few years before the United States entered the war in Europe. Hitler has reoccupied the Rhineland, and Mussolini is bragging about his conquest of Ethiopia.

"The world is an awful, restless place of late," he writes. "When will we learn to live together without constantly being at each other's throats?"

Yes, when?

Recently he has submitted an article called "Jukes, Jackasses, and Race-Horses" to a *Reader's Digest* contest and is waiting for the results. Meanwhile he's dating my mother, Lois Cline, "a very unselfish girl," who suggested revisions to the article and typed the final draft. (A typing whiz, she taught me to type by the touch method, covering the keys of our Underwood with adhesive tape so I couldn't cheat.)

Next thing you know, she's taken him home to meet her parents in Watertown, Connecticut, over Easter weekend, and he's beginning to wonder "if she might not make an ideal wife." He mentions his "esteem" for her, and her "affection" for him, and goes on to list other qualities in her that he admires—"thoughtful helpfulness," and "common good sense leavened with the proper amount of desire to do irrational things."

Like *what*, for example? He doesn't say. But the omission of juicy details and the formality of the language do not hide the fact that in his attraction for this unselfish girl he has encountered something extremely powerful and at the same time extremely dangerous. At first he doesn't know what to make of it, so he takes a rational approach—he makes a list of her good qualities, as if he were considering an applicant for admission to Columbia. He's still "enamoured" of his "freedom," he writes. But there's not one critical word about my mother, no explicit weighing of doubts on the other side of the scale, nothing to suggest that he might be better off staying single for a while. I suspect that the writing of that list was the act of a man who'd already lost all hope of making a rational decision where Lois Cline was concerned.

Between us, Anne and I have been married to other people five times. We ought to know better by now, and I haven't ruled out the possibility that, at long last, we do. We've been together for almost four years, and although you can never know for sure about these things, it feels like we're just beginning. If I were filling out a form and had to describe our relationship in the meager space provided, I'd write, "Committed, dating approx. 3x per week." Her house and mine are 1.6 miles apart; depending on the traffic, it takes between five and seven minutes to drive from one place to the other. Each of us keeps a toothbrush at the other's house, a bathrobe, a book and a few other things that were left behind, intention- ally or otherwise. A ceramic olive boat and a lawnmower are the only common property that I'm aware of. When we want to see each other, we call or e-mail to make a date. It's taken for granted that we'll spend Friday and Saturday nights together, but arrangements for those nights continue to be made in advance. When she cooks for me, she cooks the way she does for a guest; I cook for her the same way. Sometimes we cook together with minimal loss of blood. I always look forward to see- ing her and always regret having to leave her or, worse, seeing her leave me—the abrupt reconstitution of the psyche that happens when her car turns the corner at Kaune Elementary and I have to remind myself who I was and what I was doing before she arrived. Sometimes I try to imag- ine what life would be like without her, as a way of preparing myself for any eventuality. This shouldn't be hard to imagine, since I lived without her for fifty-six years. But it is, and I've almost given up trying. She will accept "I love you" from me because she knows it's true. She's told me the same thing a few times. One time I said, "I'll love you forever." She replied, "How do you know?"

In May he sees friends "properly married" and begins to entertain ideas of his own. Lois, he ventures, has more to do with those ideas than the desirability of marriage in general. "The whole affair has been so entirely need-filling and satisfactory that it has crept up on my unsuspecting heart." He doesn't actually use the L word at this point in history, prefer- ring the measured "fondness." But there's no doubt he's a goner.

They spend another weekend in Watertown at my grandparents'—
"a period so replete with moonlight through tall graceful elm trees,
sunshine over spacious fields, and the restful songs of birds at twilight
that we found it very difficult to contain our exuberance." (The reader
assumes they did.) He asks her to marry him on the condition that they
both feel the same about each other in another year. A wise woman, my
mother. If he's going to make conditions (does anyone *ever* feel the same
from one year to the next?), she's not going to come right out and say
"yes," either. But she does make it "blissfully clear" that there can be no
other answer.

Not long after getting engaged, they go to a chop suey restaurant on
111th St. in New York and then to her room to cuddle up and plan their
future. It's raining out. They talk about how they will furnish their apartment. After he writes "the book of the century," money won't be a problem. Somewhere along the way, they'll give birth to red-haired twins.

No other intimate details are provided, but it's implied that throughout the year of their engagement, they parted after every date to sleep
separately. House rules? Their own standards of propriety? Somebody
else's? He kisses her good night, takes the stairs, steps out into the rain,
and walks the half mile to his apartment. Even the dirty streets of uptown Manhattan shine with promise.

I'm moved by my father's account of that rainy night when he and my
mother, in their desire for each other and their untrammeled innocence
of all it implied, sat in her room and made their plans. There's part of me
that wants to play the cynic and warn him, like an older brother, about
the twin snares of marriage and family. Another part wants to reach
across the seventy years that have passed since then and say to my par-
ents-to-be, "Go, children, and be happy." This was their moment of pure
bliss, when the idea of living together first took shape—long before the
humdrum facts of domestic life arose. At least they had their moment.
Without such moments, who would ever take on the monumental work
of having a family and making a home?

The funny thing is, for all my years and experience, I'm hardly less excited and hopeful about my future with Anne than my father was about his prospects in 1936. He was only twenty-seven then—exactly my age when I first married. He was full of love and hope (I was, too). He was mostly unscarred by life's disappointments, although he does mention earlier in the journal that there were one or two "other ones" before my mother who, unlike her, tore at his "vitals." (My first girlfriend tore at my vitals for seven years before someone else "got her pregnant," although since then I've come to admit that she got herself pregnant at the same time.) Having never been married before, he couldn't have known any better what he was getting into than you can know what it means, for example, to be a parent before your first child is born. But the fact that I've been there and done that doesn't keep me from wanting to go to some other place, a place never visited before, and do something else. What I know about loss, more or less than what other people know, isn't nearly enough to keep me from climbing out on that precarious limb once again. My expectations may have changed since that first girlfriend sent me her Dear John letter, postmarked in faraway St. Louis, Missouri, asking me not to write to her again. But the tireless longing to have and belong to one other person hasn't abandoned me yet.

Later that summer. They're sitting on the veranda of the church rectory in Watertown with my grandparents, and my father has been waiting nervously all evening for a break in the conversation to tell them the news. He's confident that my grandfather will be pleased, less sure about my grandmother's response.

"Folks," he says, trying to sound as casual as possible, "how would you like to be let in on a deep, dark secret?"

What he delivers next is an announcement, not a petition. The days of asking your prospective father-in-law for his daughter's hand in marriage are over.

"Well!" says my grandfather in his mock-serious way. "Have you given this matter serious consideration? Do you love each other?"

Both men are aware of the need for love and serious consideration, both. After all, love is serious business. At the same time, they do their gentlemanly best to keep things light.

"Well, I don't know," is all my grandmother has to say. I'll never know what she was thinking, but it might have had something to do with my father's less-than-great expectations as a college admissions officer. She herself had dropped down the social scale a couple of notches to marry my grandfather, an Episcopalian minister, who couldn't have made much money. She may have wished her daughter to escape a similar fate. Nevertheless, both she and my grandfather accept the news "with great fortitude."

My parents want to keep their engagement a secret from the rest of the world until the first of the year, when they plan to announce "the pending disaster," as my father calls it—a weak attempt at sarcasm to save himself from the rising tide of sentiment. "Now that I have brought my hesitant, analytical self to the point of definitely deciding to marry, Lois has grown dearer and more indispensable to my existence by incredible leaps and bounds."

Here, perhaps without recognizing it as such, he's touched a thorny issue. How is it that one's existence can be whole and independent up to a point, and from that point on dependent on the existence of another? Certainly the other person is "dear" to you; otherwise you wouldn't even consider joining your life with theirs. But is he or she really "indispensable"? It's one thing to say, "I want to live with you," another to say, "I can't live without you." And in that shift from the affirmative to the negative, love's deception lies. The trouble is—one of the troubles, anyway—once you've come believe that another person is indispensable, they tend to become just that. My father's remark about "the pending disaster," however playfully sarcastic, shows that he was not innocent of the threat that marriage posed to his "freedom," by which he certainly meant more than just sexual freedom. I can't help wondering what else he was sacrificing that summer night in Connecticut when he so bravely stood before my grandparents and announced the future.

Anne and I both understand the difficulty of maintaining a private life outside of our shared privacy, and that's just the first issue between two people who are used to spending lots of time alone—that is, alone without the other. It's been ten years since I lived with a woman, so long that I can't even remember what that means or guess if it means the same kinds of things from one time to the next. One would hope not, but hope can be a treacherous ally. At our age, sixty, maybe the time has come to give up hope once and for all, linked as it is to an uncertain and rapidly shrinking future. But giving up hope won't do us any good if we can't give up its companion, fear, at the same time.

Partly because she will move into my house, rather than the other way around, her life and habits are in greater danger of being compromised by the move than mine. For that reason we agreed that she will have her own self-contained apartment, attached to the house, with a private entrance, a kitchen, a full bath, a ten-foot-long closet. It's the best room in the house, where I will be admitted by invitation only. Clearly, I'm willing to do just about anything to protect her privacy, her conviction of being one person, not two, within a context that tends to blur the lines of individuality at best and obliterate them, at worst. I've already painted the living room Chai Latte and the bedroom Ansonia Peach, two colors that might have escaped my attention altogether if not for her. In my eagerness to please and accommodate, will I remember to please myself, too?

In October his *Reader's Digest* article, one of 43,000 submitted, is returned to him with a note saying it made it to the final round of judging before it was turned down. No matter. He intends to write "for the sheer love of writing."

The wedding is set for July. "We love each other so ardently that our married life cannot fail to be the sort of which I have dreamed. . . . I do so yearn for the day when we shall be settled in our cozy apartment [and] we won't have to be always going away from each other (particularly at bedtime)."

Cozy, it was. After I was born, my parents slept on a foldout couch in the living room of our apartment, with no door between them and their three children. From then until my sisters moved away, they never had a bedroom of their own. My mother dressed in my sisters' bedroom. My father dressed from a closet in the hallway, keeping the closet door open to spare his daughters from the sight of a naked man. Talk about loss of privacy!

They're busy making plans and attending social occasions that winter. Before making the great leap into marriage, he strives to put his affairs in order, "much as we used to round up the piles of corn at home." My father hardly ever spoke about his childhood on the farm in West Virginia, one that he preferred to forget. Toward the end of the year he visits his mother, Minnie Sherwood, a farmwoman I met only a few times and remember mainly for her kindness to me, her devoted reading of the Bible, and her biscuits. He finds her well, but she misses her children terribly. This is something he will not fully understand, he says, until he has grown old himself and his own children have left home—and maybe not even then, he speculates, "because I am a man."

They choose furniture, look for an apartment, decide who will get invitations and who announcements. He wants to buy a new car: Ford or Plymouth? It will cost about $600, which will put a strain on their finances for a while, but my mother will go along with him, make the necessary sacrifices. She's "a real pal," he writes. She will be "a great stabilizer" in his life. Nowhere does he suggest that stabilization might be anything other than a good thing.

This is a small town; you can't help running into people. But in the past four years, with one qualified exception, Anne and I have never met accidentally. The exception happened one afternoon when we were driving in opposite directions on Osage Avenue. I didn't recognize her car as it approached, a light blue four-door like many others in town. (Anne's son Kalu, now away at college, said, "It looks like somebody's mother's car.") Our eyes met, and for an instant she might have been a beautiful stranger in a passing car who happened to return my look in a way that expressed mild interest in my interest, until, after we had passed, it hit me that the beauty of that particular face, too briefly there and gone, was one that I could no longer respond to for its beauty alone, that is, apart from all the other complex feelings that it excites in me and always will no matter what happens from now on. Did she catch me giving her the predatory-male eye before I realized who she was? Each of us thought in that moment of delayed recognition about turning around and overtaking the other to see what they were up to (we don't have cell phones), but as properly busy people and the custodians of each other's privacy, we chose instead to go on about our business—she to the post office, I to Home Depot—and explore the deeper meanings of that sighting in our good sweet time.

Full disclosure: Osage Avenue isn't the direct route from my place to Home Depot. I'd decided to stop by her place and see what she was up to, although it wasn't any of my business. We know and trust each other well enough that dropping in is always a pleasant surprise for the one who's dropped in on, which I believe is one sign of a maturing relationship. No need to call ahead. Never once when I dropped in has she been less than happy to see me; she only gets unhappy when I apologize for dropping in, which I often do, and which always pisses her off for reasons that I pretend to understand but really don't. I want her to know that I know that her privacy has been violated in a small way. She wants me to know—what?—that to apologize for wanting to see her is a dull formality, a gesture less than intimate?

Of course, everything will change after she moves in, if we go actually through with it. We will constantly be running into each other, but without the same surprise of that afternoon on Osage, without quite the same rush of joy that I feel now when I'm alone in my house and hear footsteps in the kitchen and know that only one person besides the cat ever enters this house without knocking. When I turn the corner and suddenly come face to face with another human being, I will not jump out of my skin the way I did, time after time, when a friend was living here last year. Rather than making dates to see each other, she and I will make dates to be apart, enforced breaks from each other's company. That won't be easy, not just because we'll be living in the same house, but because the same gravity that brought us together in the first place keeps us no farther than arm's length apart when we're in the same house, hers or mine. The danger is that, in one house, our life together will become one continuous intrusion. If that ever happens, at least I won't be as inclined to apologize as I am now.

They dine at the oyster bar in Grand Central Station before he goes on an upstate admissions trip, leaving her in tears. When he returns, she flies into his arms: "It seemed that we could not hold each other close enough or long enough." With nothing short of "absolute certainty," he knows that "the step we are taking is going to be the best thing that could happen to both of us." All that keeps him from being the happiest man alive is the auto strike in Detroit, which is delaying delivery of his new Plymouth. One would never suspect at this point in the narrative that the world at large is on the brink of its own disaster.

It may just be my skeptical frame of mind, but whenever someone claims to be absolutely certain of something, I have to assume they're not—otherwise they wouldn't feel compelled to advertise it. I can't think of many things that will throw a man into a more intense state of uncertainty than getting married, short of going to war, and each of us deals with it differently. My father is whistling in the dark.

The first time I got married, it was no big deal, or so I thought: this is just something that happens to people, like getting a job, not to be any more avidly sought after than it is to be avidly avoided. The second time, I was scared half to death and did it anyway because I was in love with the idea of living recklessly for at least once in my life. Both times, "certainty" was the farthest thing from my mind, and even now, on the verge of doing something serious again, I don't expect that certainty will overtake me any time soon.

Warm weather is some consolation for the fact that the Plymouth still hasn't arrived. As the wedding approaches, he looks back over the past year, its "matchless joys of planning and anticipation"—as much as to say that the life so keenly anticipated will never match his expectations for it.

"And then before we knew it the great day was upon us."

The sky has the weight and color of lead. Jacob Clute, my mother's mother's father, thinks "it might burn off," a remark my father often repeated to us, his children, when it was raining or about to rain. I'm more likely to quote a friend of mine who says, "It's always darkest before things really get bad." My father's optimism against my pessimism. His corniness against my sarcasm. Over time I've come to see that he and I are so precisely north and south that we line up along a common meridian.

This time, Great-Grandfather is right. The sun finally shines through the leaden clouds. Family and friends gather in the church (only my uncle Fred and his wife have shown up from my father's distant side of the family). Standing at the head of the aisle waiting for his bride, my father feels exultant, even transcendent: "Ever so briefly, I seemed to have ceased to be one of the chief actors in this little romantic drama and to have been removed into objective contemplation of the picture. How wonderful all the world seemed!" Then my mother is standing at his side—"fresh, tremulous and beautiful as a dewy white rose in the morning sunlight." My grandfather reads the service "with moving sincerity," and the deed is done.

The joys and responsibilities of marriage being what they are, he doesn't get around to writing this account of the wedding until three months later. In the same entry, he mentions "an increasingly complicated world situation of which no one can foresee the ultimate outcome."

Maybe we're taking all of this too seriously. The other day Anne learned of a young woman who's planning a theme wedding in Las Vegas, Nevada, the world's capital of ill-conceived marriages. The theme is music, since the groom is a rock musician. The ceremony will be conducted by the Reverend Elvis Presley. After carefully considering what she'll wear, the bride chose an old-fashioned gown, voluminous and ornate, perhaps very much like the dress my mother got married in, except this one is made of black leather.

"They're thinking of it as a starter marriage," says Anne. "The wedding will be very expensive. The bride's mother told her, 'You can get married as many times as you want. But you'll only get one wedding out of me.'"

Maybe they, our children's generation, have the right idea—or at least a more realistic idea than the one our parents had, which was to get together with one person and stay with them forever. People are living longer these days. (My parents died in their early seventies, which used to be the norm.) It's unreasonable to expect two people to live together happily all of their adult lives, especially if they marry in their twenties. We—she and I—don't deceive ourselves that living together will be any easier, any less demanding of attention and commitment, any more forgiving of harm or neglect than its admittedly more formidable big sister, marriage. The undoing of such an arrangement, if it comes to that, will be no less painful than divorce. At our age, moving in together could well turn into a permanent arrangement—permanent, that is, until one or the other of us dies, the biological statute of limitations honored in traditional wedding ceremonies. But one of the great advantages of getting together with someone after the age of sixty is that forever doesn't seem as impossibly long as it used to. With any luck, forever might just be doable.

My father was the most loving and devoted of husbands. He did his best to provide for his family, although my mother made no secret of the fact that she wanted more. He never said an angry word to her within my hearing. He didn't cheat on her or go out drinking with "cronies," as he called them, although he enjoyed a social life through his work that held no interest for her. After they finally got a bedroom of their own, they slept in separate beds. My mother said that he sometimes "visited" her there (this, after the premarital year of wishing for a time when they would never again have to sleep separately). If he was less than content, I never heard a word of it while my mother was alive, and only once, after she died, did he confide to me the shocking notion that "a man" could live just as happily alone as he could with a woman. The implication, which he may not have intended, was that a woman could not.

He was a loving father, too, although what I remember best are the things about me that disappointed him—that I didn't take to tennis with his enthusiasm, that I gave up the academic career that my education had prepared me for, that I wasn't friendlier—which probably says more about me than him. If he was curious about my relationships with women, he never let on. He sometimes looked surreptitiously at other women in public—I have an image of him eyeing a salesgirl in a downtown department store while I was trying on shoes. He would quote the conventional wisdom, "You can't live with them, and you can't live without them," although he had chosen to live, not with "them," but with one and only one. He liked to quote Thoreau: "The mass of men live lives of quiet desperation."

My father died two years after my mother, alone in his apartment in Connecticut, where they'd moved after he retired. He seemed to be getting stronger after the devastation of losing her, indispensable though she had been to his existence. Shortly before he died he wrote to me that he was keeping busy, reading Carl Sandburg's biography of Lincoln, playing tennis, trying to eat better. He even had "a couple of girlfriends."

After the funeral and the reception, my sisters and I were cleaning out his apartment when a woman called, a person unknown to any of us, and asked if she could drop in and pay her respects. She came to the door, a woman in her sixties wearing a white suit, a color my mother never would have dreamed of wearing because it soiled easily and required dry cleaning—one of the girlfriends. She apologized for not coming to the service or the reception—not that she'd been invited—and told us about a road trip that she and my father had taken in New England to see the autumn "foliage," as he called it. A complete stranger, she stood there in tears, bearing witness to their love before us, his astonished children. The furniture had already been removed, so there was no place for her to sit.

The next day, I found a small spiral notebook among his possessions with only one incomplete sentence written in it, as if he had intended to start writing again after a lifetime of tending to other business and was giving himself a first, tentative assignment: "Most prized possession—wedding ring."

The Correct Bird

SOMEONE LEFT A RELIGIOUS PAMPHLET ON THE DOOR while I was at work. The cover is a watercolor collage of the Works of Man—Khufu's pyramid at Giza, the moon landing, test tubes and laboratory flasks floating in a blue ether, and the words, "All Suffering Will End Soon." I stick it on my new refrigerator next to a magnetic cutout of Michelangelo's David, where it will lend itself to interpretation in the crucial weeks ahead. Are we being consoled or warned?

Until last week David occupied Anne's refrigerator, but now she's in the process of moving in with me along with all her stuff, everything that can't be sold or thrown away or left behind at her house, which she plans to rent partially furnished. Before last week my refrigerator never had anything on it except the recycling calendar—the red weeks and the green weeks, respectively, reminding me when and when not to put out the recycling. The calendar never concerned me much until now. When I saw it at all, I saw it as an indication that someone lived here and was taking care of the place. But next to David and the Works of Man it seems awfully dull, not up to new-refrigerator-door standards, so I move it to the side of the microwave where it's not as likely to be seen.

We lie awake in the middle of the night talking about vacuum cleaners. Hers was bought new from a vacuum cleaner dealer, but it swallowed something it couldn't digest and broke down, so now it will only run for about five minutes at a time before shutting itself off. The owner's manual says that the ability to shut itself off before catching fire is one of the special features of this machine.

"Do you *like* your vacuum cleaner?" I inquire earnestly. Her lovely back is turned toward me and longs to be touched. My hand moves up her spinal column to the slight concavity at the base of her skull, a doorway to the medulla oblongata. I've heard that you can put someone to sleep by massaging them there, and with a million things to do, sleep is what we need most.

"I liked it when it worked. It was the best vacuum cleaner I've ever had."

"Why not get it fixed?"

"The guy said it would cost $250. That's nearly half what I paid for it."

"Yeah, but where can you get a vacuum cleaner as good as yours for $250?"

Ten or twenty minutes pass in which neither of us speaks. It's hard to gage the passing of time in the dark. Thanks to a light-sensitive mechanism, the birds in my Audubon Society wall clock, a present from a former wife, do not sing in the dark. Even if they did, it's been years since they sang at their appointed hours—the great horned owl at noon and midnight, et cetera. Every time the batteries die or the time changes, the birds play musical chairs with the hours, and I can't know for sure what time it is without looking at the clock.

"What about *your* vacuum cleaner?"

"The Eureka? I got it for ten dollars at a yard sale. It only does floors."

"Do you think we could get along with just one vacuum cleaner?"

Unanswered, the question hangs ominously in the dark between us. After a night of restless sleep, I wake to the faint song of a northern cardinal, a bird that doesn't live in this part of the country, but I remember them from my childhood in the East. Due to the light-sensitive mechanism, the birds in the clock sing only faintly when the room is dimly lit, at dawn and dusk. The brighter it gets, the louder they sing.

Before Anne started moving in, the only picture on the wall was an oil painting by my daughter Hannah of a wooden stool against a blue wall in an otherwise empty room, a picture that only emphasized the blankness of the walls around it. The actual stool, the model for the painting, was probably the first new piece of furniture I'd ever owned, when I was living in a house that I and Hannah's mother built with salvaged materials—adobe bricks from a ruined farmhouse, window sashes from a salvage yard, floor boards from a vacant high school gymnasium. Besides that stool, the house may not have had another single new, store-bought thing in it.

I never chose sparseness over abundance. It just didn't occur to me to fill up the empty places any more than it occurred to me to decorate the refrigerator door. To that extent, my aesthetic doesn't qualify as an aesthetic at all. I never noticed the absence of things around me, as friends did, but I do notice the absence of that absence, now that it's quickly disappearing.

An Etruscan horse, blue stormclouds over purple foothills, a pair of skeletons holding hands in outer space. Each picture must find a home on the blank walls that is particularly its own, not too high or too low, too far left or right. It takes two people to hang a picture, I discover, one to hold it and the other to direct. Then the holder becomes the director and vice versa until a compromise is met. If the picture is in the wrong place or has no place in the house at all, we may not know it right away, but we'll know it within a few days, and each of us will know it independently before we admit it to each other.

I don't have much experience looking at pictures, so it's hard to say if I like the Etruscan horse, the stormclouds, and the skeletons for themselves or because they came with Anne. But I do like them. They give me a pleasure that's recognizable, if not immediately placeable, like the face of someone you used to know but whose name and circumstances you've since forgotten. Once they've been hung, I hardly resent the loss of absence that they represent, which leads me to wonder what other kinds of sparseness I might be prepared to live without in the future.

She thinks I don't have enough books.

"How can someone who's a writer not have any books?"

"I do have books. But only the ones I plan to read again. What—am I supposed to keep them for decoration?"

I think she has too many books. For days I've been running truck-loads of books from her place to mine, building shelves and stacking boxes wherever I can find a few cubic feet of unoccupied space.

"*Answers to Questions: Five Thousand Curious Facts for Inquiring Minds.* How long has it been since you looked at this one?"

"I'd keep it even if I never looked at it. You never know when you might need to answer a question."

I flip through the five thousand questions and find this one: "Do you know why Greenland is named Greenland?"

"Why?"

"'Upon his return to Norway in AD 985, Eric the Red gave the new country that name in order to make people more willing to go there.' I didn't know that, did you?"

"See? That's why you need more books."

She puts an ad in the paper and another on craigslist to rent her house. First and last month's rent plus a deposit. No smoking, period. No pets of any description. ("People will whine and beg and tell you they have the best-behaved dog in the world," I tell her. "Don't believe them.") No disabled vehicles in the driveway with oil slowly dripping into a hubcap. No more than three unrelated tenants. No loud parties after ten at night.

"It's best to take a hard line. After they move in, they're going to do anything they want, anyway."

Immediately she receives a reply on craigslist from Daniel Buck, an Englishman whose employer, the Japan Tobacco Company, is transfer-ring him to Santa Fe. All terms stated in the ad are acceptable, writes Mr. Buck. The company is going to pay his rent while he's here by means of a monthly bank draft. Attached to his e-mail is a photograph of Daniel in mortarboard and gown posing for a graduation photo in a misty English courtyard. The English in the letter is a little strange for an Englishman, but he looks very clean and sober, a little overweight, just the sort of responsible fellow you'd want living in your house. Standing next to him is an unidentified young woman, also in cap and gown, equally clean and sober, who may or may not be his girlfriend and may or may not be coming with him to the United States. No way of knowing except to ask. Has he read the stipulation about no smoking? And what is Japan Tobacco doing in our small, laid-back provincial capital, where the two major industries are state government and massage therapy?

Anne e-mails Daniel Buck with these and other questions and receives a neat list of answers to questions that she didn't ask. Meanwhile, three college girls come to look at the house and are absolutely thrilled with it. They don't smoke. They have no pets, well behaved or otherwise. And their check clears.

"This raft is getting very close to the edge of the falls," says Anne.

Clearly, having come this far together, there's no longer any hope of reaching shore or paddling back upstream to the separate lives we are about to leave behind. We can barely imagine, much less name, the consequences that have already been set in motion. It seems highly unlikely, for example, that in the life to come I will come home from work, open my lavishly decorated refrigerator door, smear some peanut butter and jelly between two slices of bread, pop a beer, and collapse in front of the evening news without at least asking if she wants some, too. As close to the edge as we've come, we might be talking conscientiously about the long-term implications of our new arrangement. Instead, we talk about *things* and where to put them.

"What do you think about the rug that's in my living room going in the bedroom?"

"Will it fit?"

"I don't know. I wrote down the measurements somewhere."

"Did you measure the bedroom?"

"No, that's something I need to do. Then I have to find where I wrote down the measurements for the rug."

"It might be simpler just to move the rug."

"Right. I guess it's coming to that."

On a back street between her house and mine, an alternate route that she has only learned recently, Anne finds a yard sale and buys a Kirby vacuum cleaner for $5. It must be at least twenty-five years old, but it has attachments for vacuuming drapes and furniture and getting under the bed. Not only that, it runs without shutting itself off every five minutes, filling the air with a powerful smell of raw electrical energy. Of course, I'm happy for her—for us—but concerned that my old standby, the Eureka, is in danger of being replaced by the older, heavier, cheaper, more versatile machine. With cloying affection, she calls the new vacuum "Kirby," and for the next few days it's nothing but Kirby this and Kirby that.

"I don't know if I'm ready to give up the Eureka just yet," I tell her. "All of this is happening so fast. Maybe I'll put it out in the shed for a while until we see how Kirby works out."

Sure enough, Kirby is everything she's ever wanted in a vacuum cleaner. But instead of putting the Eureka in the shed with the lowly garden tools, I hide it in my office closet, where I can get it out and secretly vacuum the house when she's not here—a small infidelity, but one, I believe, that's in the best interests of the commonwealth.

Anne makes a quick trip to California to visit her mother, leaving me at home to organize our possessions and contemplate the puzzling message about suffering on the refrigerator door.

"Call me when you get home," I say out of habit when I talk to her on the telephone.

"What do you mean? I live with you."

"Of course you do. Don't think I've forgotten."

There it is staring me in the face every time I go to make a peanut butter sandwich. Can it be saying that death will come for us soon, and then we won't have to suffer any more? That something else is going to happen, something dramatic, and from then on, even though we're still alive, we won't have to suffer? A life after death without suffering? None of the above? Maybe it's neither a promise nor a threat, but a reminder. Suffering and nonsuffering alike will end soon; we'd better do all we can of both while there's time.

Wrapped in its shining skin of reticulated steel, the Frigidaire is only the second new refrigerator I've ever owned. It replaces an almond-colored GE that was still working fine when they hauled it off, supposedly to drain the freon and salvage the metal parts. When you live with a major appliance for nineteen years, it's hard not to feel a pang of regret when you see it loaded unceremoniously by a couple of ruffians who couldn't care less about a refrigerator, working or not, whose time has come and gone. But it was too small for a household that's about to double in size, and besides, it was almond.

There was a time when the idea of owning new kitchen appliances, with their implications of domestic stasis, threw me into a panic. (Once I broke off an engagement when my fiancée's parents threw a party and presented us with an electric rotisserie big enough to roast a yearling calf.) Now I'm just grateful to have a refrigerator that keeps things cold and is pleasant to look at. Fingerprints are hard to remove from its shining surface, and it makes strange noises from time to time, like a dog barking in the distance. Why it barks at certain times and not others is impossible to say, but I have more important things to do than call the manufacturer and complain that my new refrigerator is barking under warranty. I hardly noticed it when Anne was in the house, but it's been quite pronounced since she went away—more so, I suspect, than if she had never come here at all. I grew used to silence in my years of being single, but now the silence has grown uncomfortably loud.

When she returns, only two days remain before the three college girls will take full possession of her house. We lie awake in the night, mentally packing the last few boxes, running ethernet cables through the crawl space, planning strategy for the War of the Barbecues. Everything must go somewhere, that much is certain. Her fennel seeds and mine will mingle in a single ziplock baggie.

"The palm trees are wearing terrycloth bathrobes," she says later, when both of us have been asleep.

More time passes. I say, "They probably stole them from the hotel."

She laughs, which means that she knows that I know that she knows what I mean.

Rain and thunder before dawn—what my father used to call "an equinoctial storm." From now on the earth will lean away from the sun, and we have no choice but to lean with it. In the clouded light of morning the northern cardinal fails to waken, and the first bird of morning is the downy woodpecker, a bird who does, in fact, live in these mountains.

"What time is it?"

"I don't know. The downy woodpecker used to be four o'clock, but that was a long time ago."

"You mean the birds sing at the wrong time?"

"You'll get used to it."

"Can't it be fixed?"

"I suppose so. But why bother?"

Later that day she takes the clock down from the wall and reads the instructions on the back, which end with a stern warning: "You must follow these instructions to reset properly or you will not hear the correct melody with the correct bird." When she's done replacing the batteries and following the instructions to the letter, the birds continue to sing at the wrong time, but at least they're consistently, unanimously wrong. And there's always a chance that when the time changes next month, they'll get it right on their own.

A native New Yorker, Tom Ireland moved to New Mexico in 1971 to live at Lama Foundation. Lama published his first book, *Mostly Mules*, the account of a trying journey by mule through Rio Arriba. For years he worked as a builder, rancher, and animal trainer, avoiding steady employment until the age of forty. Since 1987 he's been an editor at the Office of Archaeological Studies, a state agency. The author of four books of nonfiction, he has an MFA in writing from Stanford and received an NEA literary grant and a Jeffrey E. Smith Prize. More information on his work is available at tomireland.net.

Photograph by Hannah Ireland

OTHER TITLES BY TRES CHICAS BOOKS

Rice
Joan Logghe, 2004

Water Shed
Renée Gregorio, 2004

Just Outside the Frame: Poets from the Santa Fe Poetry Broadside
edited by Miriam Bobkoff and Miriam Sagan, 2005

Big Thank You
JB Bryan, 2006

Water Shining Beyond the Fields
John Brandi, 2006

The Sound a Raven Makes
Sawnie Morris   Michelle Holland   Catherine Ferguson, 2006
WINNER OF THE 2007 NEW MEXICO BOOK AWARD FOR POETRY

Gossip
Miriam Sagan, 2007

Pinning the Bird to the Wall
Devon Miller-Duggan, 2008

All Tres Chicas Book titles are available directly from the publishers at
reneeclaire@cybermesa.com
joanlogghe@hotmail.com
msagan1035@aol.com
or on the web at Amazon.com
& Small Press Distribution at spdbooks.org

Kali is an aspect of the great goddess Devi, the most complex and powerful of the goddesses. Kali is one of the fiercer aspects of Devi, but nonetheless as Shiva's consort, she represents female energy. Kali's aspect is destructive and all-pervading, as she represents the power or energy of time. Her four arms represent the four directions of space identified with the complete cycle of time. Kali is beyond time, beyond fear . . . her giving hand shows she is the giver of bliss. Because she represents a stage beyond all attachment, she appears fearful to us. So, she has a dual aspect— both destroyer of all that exists and the giver of eternal peace.

This image is from drawings by women of Mithila, India.